The Game That Was

The George Brace Baseball Photo Collection

Richard Cahan

and

Mark Jacob

CB

CONTEMPORARY BOOKS

A TRIBUNE NEW MEDIA/EDUCATION COMPANY

Library of Congress Cataloging-in-Publication Data

Cahan, Richard.
     The game that was : the George Brace baseball photo collection /
Richard Cahan and Mark Jacob.
          p.   cm.
     Includes bibliographical references and index.
     ISBN 0-8092-3200-6
     1. Baseball—United States—History—Pictorial works.   I. Jacob,
Mark.   II. Title.
GV863.A1C35   1996
796.357′0973′022—dc20   95-47535
                                                                CIP

Interior design by Kim Bartko

Published by Contemporary Books, Inc.
Two Prudential Plaza, Chicago, Illinois 60601-6790
Manufactured in the United States of America
International Standard Book Number: 0-8092-3200-6
10   9   8   7   6   5   4   3   2   1

For my mother, Dorothy, who never threw out my baseball cards

—Richard Cahan

For my mother, Jane, a lifelong Tigers fan and brilliant softball coach, and for my father, John, who always threw me pitches I could hit

—Mark Jacob

CONTENTS

ACKNOWLEDGMENTS

The authors wish to thank Mary Brace and Debbie Miller, who printed the pictures and found many hidden treasures.

Ed McGregor and Steve Green opened doors with the Chicago Cubs. Former Cubs executive E. R. "Salty" Saltwell, former Cubs groundskeeper Roy "Cotton" Bogren, 1940s White Sox batboy Pete Pervan, and veteran baseball photographer Don Wingfield took us back to an era when baseball was America's dream game.

Baseball experts Joseph McCarthy Jr., Ralph Moses, John Thorn, Richard Lindberg, Marc Okkonen, Eddie Gold, Gil Lande, and Bob Garfinkle provided many details that help make this book work. Don Gutteridge, Woody English, Billy Jurges, Ernie Banks, Bob Feller, and Milt Gaston shared big league memories. Photo conservator Dan Cochrane was a valuable consultant.

Chicago Sun-Times colleagues Norm Schaefer, Tom Cruze, Tom McNamee, John Grochowski, Jim Montalbano, Dom Najolia, and Michael Arnold helped with design ideas, edited drafts, and provided hard-to-find research material.

Richard Cahan wants to thank his wife, Cate, and the children who make his home run: Aaron, Claire, Elie, and Glenn. He is indebted to his sister, Carol Nazarian, and brother, David; friends Mark Adler and Dennis Fertig; and—of course—the baseball buddies: Paul Motenko, Jim Phillips, Mike Ross, Garry Chankin, and Peter Korn.

Mark Jacob thanks his wife, Lisa, and his daughters, Maureen and Katherine, for their patience, support, and sense of humor. Brothers Tim, Paul, and Matt and sisters Kathleen Richman and Anne Adams have always been in his cheering section.

George Brace wants to remember his comrades killed in World War II, including his brother Leonard. He thanks Tony Inzerillo, who has donated photos to keep the Brace collection current, and Bill McAllister and Bill Loughman, who have collaborated with him on baseball projects for years. Brace also thanks his family: wife Agnes, son John, his late daughter Kathleen, and daughter Mary, who now manages the collection.

Finally, the authors are grateful to their agents, Michael Antonello and Marshall Krolick, who believed in the project, and the editors and artists at Contemporary Books, especially Kim Bartko and Dawn Barker, who brought it all together.

ABOUT THE PHOTOS

This book was more than 60 years in the making. The use of vintage large-format negatives with modern electronic darkroom techniques means these photographs are being printed with a quality not possible in years past. Latent shadow details have been returned, and underexposed portions of negatives have been restored. Much of the original retouching has been left on these pictures, some of it rather crude; the photo on page 93 is a good example. We think the retouching hearkens back to the period when the pictures were taken. In certain cases, 60-year-old fingerprints and other smudges have been removed in the electronic darkroom, always with the goal of restoring the negatives' original glory.

George Brace and his mentor, George Burke, began their baseball photo project in 1929. Although Brace continued through the 1993 season, the focus of this book is the period through 1960—the last year before the major leagues expanded beyond their original 16 teams and, coincidentally, the time Brace switched from black-and-white to color photography. Thus, the book focuses on players whose careers were established by the end of the 1950s. All identifications in the captions are left-to-right unless otherwise indicated.

Shortstop Frank Crosetti stands at the edge of the dugout with his bandaged glove as the Yankees prepare for the start of the 1938 World Series at Wrigley Field. The Yanks beat the Cubs, four games to none.

"This ball—this symbol; is it worth a man's whole life?"

—BRANCH RICKEY

THE VISION

How a studio photographer named George Burke and his apprentice, George Brace, amassed the nation's finest private collection of baseball photographs

GEORGE BRACE HAS SEEN IT ALL, and so has his camera. As a teenager, he sat between Babe Ruth and Lou Gehrig in the Yankees clubhouse. He was at baseball's first All-Star Game, saw Ruth's "Called Shot," and joined Bob Feller in the dugout before Feller's Opening Day no-hitter in 1940. He photographed Jackie Robinson during his debut season and has chronicled the rise and fall of almost every major league ballplayer since 1929.

SOME OF BRACE'S WORK IS PUBLISHED IN MAGAZINES; some is in the collection of the National Baseball Hall of Fame in Cooperstown, New York. The best of his work, thousands of intimate, beguiling, behind-the-scenes photos of baseball and its biggest stars, has remained largely unknown . . . until now.

Brace's collection—a massive archive with hundreds of thousands of negatives—depicts more than 10,000 players. He has photographed about 200 Hall of Famers as well as players who never even got to bat. The photos, particularly the old black-and-whites, are warm, unpretentious portraits of a lost age when players had the time and the inclination to mug for the camera, when stars were not too aloof to chat with a young photographer.

Brace, along with his mentor, George Burke, photographed baseball from an unusual perspective: not as a sporting event but as a social event. They paid close attention to the players warming up, the trainers, the families, and the fans. They focused on the pageantry of the game, taking pictures of batboys, mascots, groundskeepers, and even parking lot policemen. "Anything in uniform," Brace says. "If it was baseball, we photographed it."

This is a story not of hits, runs, and errors but of peanuts, pop-

George Brace surrounded by Indians Jeff Heath and Bob Feller on April 16, 1940, the day Feller pitched the only Opening Day no-hitter in major league history.

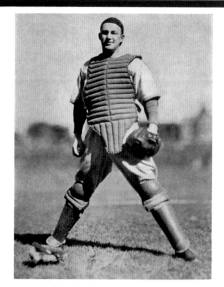

PHOTOGRAPHS
of Your Favorite Baseball Players
.25 cents EACH AND UP

Individual Photographs of all the new and some of the old Major League Players (in uniform). These photos are intended solely for baseball fans' private collections and are not to be used for any commercial purpose.

Also, many group photos of former and present teams. A postcard will bring complete list. Would like to exchange photos of today for those of yesterday.

GEO. BURKE 847 BELMONT AVENUE 27 Years at This Location **CHICAGO, ILL.**

I carry a complete line of Kodaks, Cine Kodaks, Movie Cameras and Projectors

An advertisement in the 1941 Baseball Register. The player pictured is the Cubs' Gabby Hartnett.

George Burke pauses with Cubs pitcher Lon Warneke, his best friend among major league players. The two often went hunting together near Warneke's home in Mount Ida, Arkansas.

corn, and personalities—the game of baseball as an
American ritual.

IT BEGAN WITH A WRONG NUMBER.

Just before the 1929 season, Cubs manager Joe
McCarthy and catcher Gabby Hartnett wanted photos
of the players in street clothes, and they remembered
that the ball club had used a photographer named
Burke the previous season. So they looked in the
phone book and found George C. Burke, whose studio
was near Wrigley Field. Trouble was, he was the
wrong Burke. Francis Burke, an established baseball
photographer, had been the Cubs' official
photographer for years, but no longer. George Burke
had won the starting job.

Burke, a studio photographer with no sports
experience, jumped at the chance to work at Wrigley
Field. And he quickly arranged to become the official
photographer for the Chicago White Sox and Bears as
well.

Burke needed help and took on an assistant named
George Brace, who had answered Burke's ad offering
to trade Spalding baseball guides. Brace knew a great deal about
baseball but almost nothing about photography. In the darkroom for
the first time, he thought something had gone wrong when the film
he was developing came out without paper on the back. But he
learned quickly and with great enthusiasm. Soon he was
accompanying Burke to Wrigley Field and Comiskey Park.

"I was awed," Brace says. "Allowed to go on the field. A young
kid, 16 years old."

It was a perfect time to begin a life in baseball—an era when
Ruth and Gehrig were in their prime and the Cubs were kings of the
National League.

Burke started a portfolio of ballplayer portraits during the 1930s
and soon developed a reputation around the leagues. "I remember
him," says Bob Feller, "and I remember George Brace. They took

*Joe McCarthy, whose mistaken phone
call gave birth to the Brace collection.
The photo is stamped with the logo
of Burke's photo studio, RDM,
pronounced "radium."*

great pictures. They were always around Comiskey Park. They made a good living out of it before players realized there was money to be made."

It became a regular part of the Chicago stop for each ballplayer to pose for Burke or his young apprentice. Burke and Brace would take at least two photos: one mug shot and one action shot (a pitcher in motion or a batter swinging) of every rookie and veteran on every team. Whenever a player was traded, they would take a photo of him in his new uniform. The portraits go well beyond baseball-card photography. You can see by the expressions on the players' faces that they are not hurried, not really working. They are among friends.

Chicago was the only city to possess both an American League and a National League franchise continuously from 1929, when Burke started, to 1993, when Brace retired. They never missed a home stand and never missed a player who made a Chicago appearance. Besides doing work for the teams, they sold their portraits to *The Sporting News*, *Who's Who in the Major Leagues*, and *Baseball Digest*.

At first, Burke and Brace thought they were compiling only a portrait file. But the beauty of the game drew them into recording a world of enduring youth. The lifers—people such as Casey Stengel and Leo Durocher—grew old before their cameras but seldom lost their youthful smiles. The photographers were given a unique opportunity to open the railing gate, walk onto the field, and talk to the ballplayers. They asked Bill Terry to stand by the batting cage. They told Joe DiMaggio to move so the sun would hit him just right.

Honus Wagner was among dozens of major leaguers who stopped by Burke's photo studio near Wrigley Field to pose in a formal setting.

Perhaps more important were the pregame and off-the-field photos that Burke and Brace took for the fun of it. They photographed Ted Lyons shaving in the locker room before Ted Lyons Day, Charlie Grimm feeding a bottle to a bear cub before a Cubs game, Mule

THE CUBS PITCHERS 1929
CVENGROS OSBURNE GRAMPP BLAKE CARLSON NEHF
MALONE LAND ROOT BUSH

GEO. BURKE
PHOTO

Haas fooling around with a toy mule, and Charlie Root posing with a cowboy hat and pistol.

George Brace never forgot his roots as a fan. His photographs of life at Chicago's two ballparks are perhaps the single most unusual aspect of his work. Nothing escaped his attention. During the construction of Wrigley Field's new bleachers in 1937, he photographed everything from the planting of the ivy to the building of the scoreboard. Brace shows a changing ballpark, in the days when vendors pushed carts and fans wore straw hats and suit coats to games. He shows the first cans of beer served at Comiskey Park.

One of Burke's first group photos of the team he and Brace would cover for 64 years.

Burke and Brace befriended ballplayers. They shot photos of players at parties, in hotels, and on the streets. Burke, who went by the nickname "Piper-Heidsieck" because of his brand of champagne-flavored chewing tobacco, took frequent hunting trips with Cubs Billy Herman and Lon Warneke. He joined Lefty Grove at the spas in Hot Springs, Arkansas, and took a camera wherever he went. He also took family photographs of ballplayers when they were in town, often posing the American Leaguers in Armour Park, behind Comiskey Park, and the National Leaguers at his North Side studio. Sometimes Cubs and Sox players invited Burke and Brace to their homes. The collection grew full of images of fathers and sons playing catch, brothers as teammates and competitors, and players' wives sitting in the front row under broad-brimmed hats.

Burke, who was raised in the coal-mining town of Pennington Gap, on the western edge of Virginia, came to Chicago around 1914 at age 40 and set up RDM studio (pronounced "radium") at 847 West Belmont. He sold film and took portraits on the first floor, and he slept upstairs. Brace, hired during the 1929 season, primarily worked on the baseball files in the basement for the first couple of years.

Brace was born April 11, 1913, a line drive away from Shrewbridge Field, a high school baseball park near his home at 7336 South Aberdeen Avenue. His father, Fred, was a lumberjack from Michigan who had come to Chicago to work as a carpenter. George was the oldest of four brothers and one sister. His earliest memory is of the 1919 race riots that engulfed the city's South Side. George's mother, Margaret, harbored a black neighbor in their home for several months during the height of the violence. Decades later, the woman attended Margaret's wake.

In 1920, George Brace was bedridden for months with double pneumonia, and doctors wanted to remove several ribs to help him breathe. His mother refused, and when he recovered she encouraged him to be athletic. He took up baseball and organized the Westwood Badgers, a neighborhood amateur team that was renamed St. Adrian when it joined the Catholic Youth Organization (CYO) leagues in 1929. Brace served as publicist and reserve outfielder for the team,

Burke placed construction paper around the lens of his heavy Speed Graflex camera to shield it from the light.

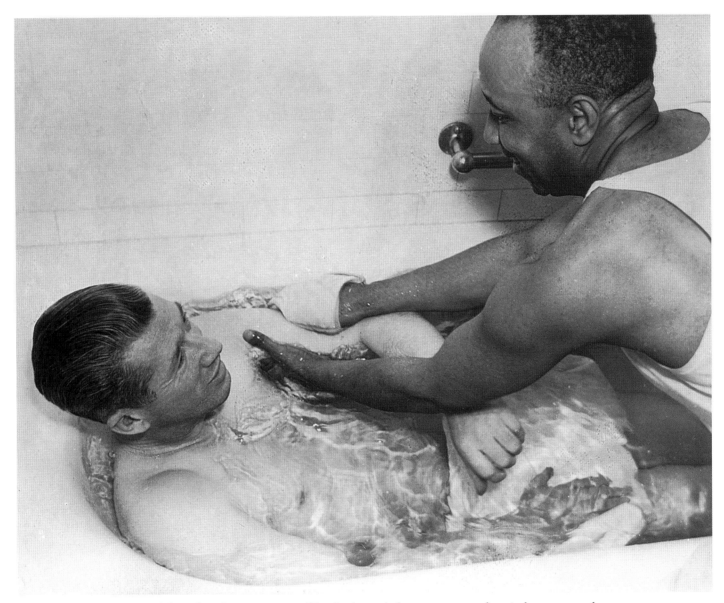

Burke took this photo of friend Lefty Grove in a Hot Springs, Arkansas, spa as the pitcher prepared for spring training. This was a favorite spot for ballplayers before spring training began.

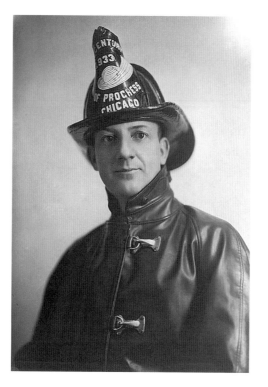

Burke photographed hundreds of employees at the 1933 Century of Progress Exposition in Chicago, including firemen and fan dancers. Shown above are fireman Henry Rohn and a dancer identified only as "Leona." Vaudeville performers populated the fair's "Bowery," a re-creation of the Lower East Side neighborhood of New York in the 1800s.

which became a city powerhouse, winning six city
championships and one national title.

In 1928, before his junior high school graduation, Brace
dropped out of school and got a job delivering Western
Union telegrams. One of his frequent stops was Al
Capone's gang headquarters, the Metropole Hotel on the
South Side. The Depression put an end to the job, but he
soon started work as a sports statistician for the CYO.

Brace was already an avid fan of baseball history by
the time he teamed up with Burke. In the mid-1920s he
would ride the streetcar downtown to copy records of
individual players at the headquarters of A. G. Spalding,
publisher of the *Spalding Guide*, the baseball bible of the
time. In the 1930s, Brace started work on a history of
baseball up to the year 1900. He received remarkable
letters from such people as George Wright, the game's first
professional, who played on the 1869 Cincinnati Red
Stockings; "Pebbly Jack" Glasscock, one of the game's first great
shortstops; and Hall of Famer Fred Clarke. Jim Delahanty, of the five
Delahanty brothers, wrote Brace: "Don't remember any real thrills.
We did not get them in the old days. Our thrills occurred on the first
and fifteenth of each month when we received our pay." Joe Gunson,
who invented the catcher's mitt during the 1880s, sent photos with
front and back views of the glove.

*Byron "Whizzer" White tried out for
the White Sox but chose pro football
instead to finance his legal career. He
ended up in the starting lineup of the
U.S. Supreme Court.*

By 1941 Brace had a file card on every man who had played in the
majors since 1876, and he proposed a book. Brace persuaded all-time
great Honus Wagner to lend his name as the author; Brace would be
the ghostwriter. But the manuscript was rejected by a publisher, who
insisted the history be brought up to the present time. Brace's history,
up to 1900, was eventually published in serial form in a baseball
magazine, *Oldtyme Baseball News*.

Brace's experience and knowledge of the game bolstered Burke's
baseball enterprise, while Burke taught Brace to be a photographer.
They both used a Speed Graflex, a portable camera with a lens that
could freeze action as well as produce beautiful portraits. It was the
favorite camera of press photographers of the age. Burke's Graflex

was huge; it held five-by-seven-inch negatives. Brace's used four-by-five negatives. Both cameras held 18 sheets of film. Burke, because of his experience, remained the more skilled of the two, but it is often hard to distinguish between their work.

The two became so close in manner and style that many players thought Brace was Burke's son. "In 1989, I went to Cooperstown and saw Ted Williams," recalls Brace. "He asked me, 'How's your dad?' After all these years."

During Burke's first few seasons, he also employed an apprentice named Norm Paulson at the ballparks for on-the-field action shots, and some of Paulson's photos became a part of the collection. After Burke trained Brace in the early 1930s, he dispatched Paulson to photograph minor league players in midwestern ballparks.

One of the few game action shots in the collection shows the Boston Braves' Elbie Fletcher playing first base during the mid-1930s. Brace made the shot from the coach's box.

Brace photographed players near the dugout or around the batting cage. "I never took a picture without asking a player's permission," he says. "One day I sat Charlie Root in a chair. I took a serious pose and said: 'Now a smile.' He said, 'Listen, young man, this is a serious game. I don't smile. This is a business. Don't ever ask me to smile.' So I never asked Charlie to smile."

Almost all players gave him the okay. Sometimes pitchers were superstitious of being photographed on the day they were pitching. "The Mad Russian," Lou Novikoff, had a phobia about being photographed on Opening Day. Rod Carew, aware of the marketing potential of his picture, refused Brace in the final seasons of his career.

But many players came to Brace; they loved to be photographed. He photographed some as many as 20 times. Burke gave each player a "sun print"—a temporary image that faded in daylight. Brace gave each player a permanent print. The players often sent the photos to their families, and the families would write for more. The photographers made photo statuettes—photos glued to plywood and then jigsawed—as keepsakes for players and produced autographed

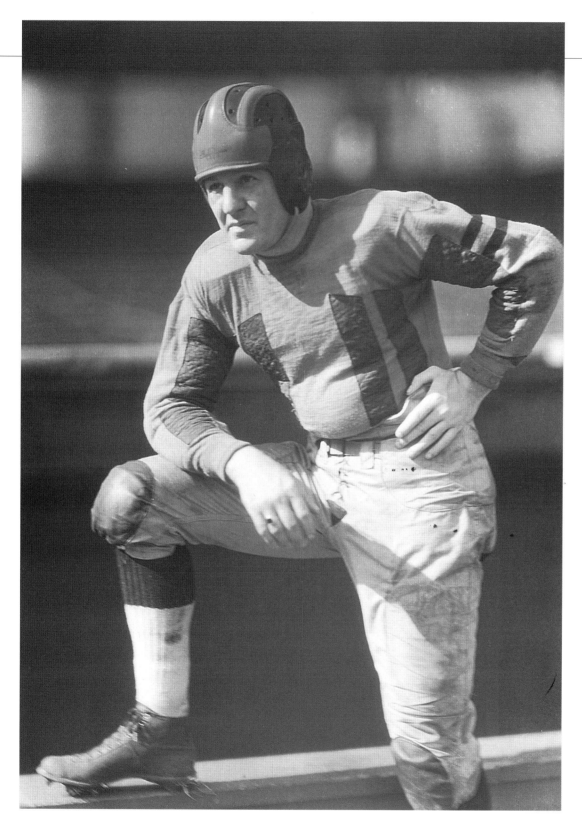

Bears running back Red Grange poses for George Burke, the team's photographer until 1948. Having photographed the Chicago Bears just before their 73–0 victory over Washington in the 1940 NFL title game, Burke came to be regarded as a lucky charm by team owner George Halas.

Burke and Brace turned their photos into eight-inch statuettes that they sold to players. Pictured here is the statuette of Cubs player Woody English.

photo cards for players to hand out. They also sold camera and movie equipment to hundreds of major leaguers.

During the 1930s, Brace took action shots from the third-base coach's box. He followed Gabby Hartnett down the third-base line after his legendary "Homer in the Gloamin'" when Hartnett was mobbed at home plate. Up until 1938, photographers were allowed to stand in the coach's boxes and were considered part of the field, just like the umpires.

"It wasn't hard," says Brace, "but you had to be on your toes because you didn't want to get hit by a ball. Mr. Burke insisted we should always wear hats. I don't know why. Maybe he thought if the ball hit us it would be deflected by our hats."

Brace married Agnes Komin on January 3, 1942. Four months later, he was drafted into the army. World War II did not slow Burke's business, and he hired a new apprentice, Richard Schneider, to fill in when Brace was away. Private Brace, stationed in western Illinois during the first part of the war, managed to sneak home to help Burke at the ballpark on weekends during the 1942 and '43 seasons.

Brace originally was assigned to the 20th Field Hospital but was transferred before that unit was sent to Europe, where it met disaster in the Battle of the Bulge. Of 200 medics and patients, only two survived the onslaught of Hitler's tanks. Brace, meanwhile, had joined the 37th Field Hospital and was sent to New Guinea in 1944, once working 72 hours straight as a surgical technician treating hundreds of wounded soldiers from a battle in the Sarmi region. Brace's youngest brother, Leonard, also serving in New Guinea, was killed in the war.

After VJ Day, Burke wired Brace that he had a field pass for the 1945 World Series, but Brace was not able to return to Chicago until November of that year. By the time he was discharged, he had two children, John and Kathleen. Mary was born a few years later. In order to support his young family, Brace got a full-time job operating a machine at Durkee Famous Foods, where he would work for 29 years. Brace volunteered for the unpopular swing shift so he could have his days free to take photos at the ballpark. The hours he spent—shooting, filing photos, and selling prints—constantly competed with family obligations. In December, when the baseball schedules were published, Brace would announce the days he needed to take off.

Burke suffered a heart attack in 1948. Unable to work, he depended on Brace to keep the business going. Burke gave him the photo collection with the understanding that Brace would pay Burke's medical bills. They renamed the business "Burke and Brace Photo," and Brace moved the collection to his home. Burke died in 1951. His body was cremated, and Brace took the ashes back to Pennington Gap. Till the day Burke died, Brace called him "Mr. Burke," and he still does.

Burke gave up the role of official photographer for the Cubs and the Sox in 1948 because of his illness, but Brace had no trouble retaining access to both teams. To this day, he remains well known at their parks.

GI George Brace with his bride, Agnes, during World War II.

To Burke, the baseball project was a business. To Brace, it has been a labor of love. He makes just enough to pay his expenses and keep the project going. Brace lost his chance at big money in 1949 when a friend sent him the rare Honus Wagner tobacco card, one of which sold decades later for $450,000. "I made a negative of the Honus Wagner card, as I always would do, and then tore the card up, as I always did," he says.

Almost all of Burke and Brace's work was at the three Chicago ballparks, Wrigley Field, old Comiskey Park, and new Comiskey. Brace never photographed the Negro Leagues, which played in Chicago. He was interested but too busy with his major league work. He did photograph several Negro League winter banquets during the early 1960s.

Brace used to arrive at the park three or four hours early, when the park felt like an open field, not an arena. Before the fans filled the

George Brace, accompanied by grandson Michael Ryan, throws out the first ball during a Cubs game in 1994.

grandstands, a stadium had a magical feel. You could hear the sound of the bat, the voices of the players, even echoes. This was the perfect time for the players to warm up, and for Brace to warm up to them.

His work completed, Brace would often leave before the national anthem was played.

This photo of Louisville Colonels minor leaguer Pee Wee Reese was taken by Burke assistant Norm Paulson after Reese became a marbles champion and before he was a star Dodgers shortstop.

BURKE AND BRACE HAD ONE PEER. Charles M. Conlon photographed baseball from 1904 until 1941. Like Brace, Conlon had to support himself in jobs other than baseball for much of his career. Conlon, of Englewood, New Jersey, worked as a newspaper copy reader. His photographs appeared in the National Portrait Gallery in 1984. They have been reproduced as baseball cards and displayed in books as fine art. Burke and Brace never met Conlon, but in the late 1930s they were collaborators in picture layouts that appeared in the Spalding baseball guides.

Conlon took formal, documentary, on-the-field photos; most of his players are stern-faced and rigid. Burke and Brace's pictures of the next generation show more of a sense of humor and encompass far more than what was on the field. Conlon left 8,000 negatives; Burke and Brace produced hundreds of thousands.

AROUND 1960, BRACE CHANGED HIS STYLE. After dropping his trusty Speed Graflex in the dugout and cracking the camera body, he decided to switch to a 35mm Zeiss Ikon camera and use color film. The results were good but not as distinctive as in his earlier years. Brace also found he had less of a connection with the players. In age and attitude, he related better to the managers, coaches, and scouts.

Still, he continued his streak. Flannels were replaced by polyester; crewcuts and clean-shaven faces gave way to long hair, bushy sideburns, and handlebar mustaches—and Brace never missed a ballplayer. Even at the age of 80, when leg problems made it difficult for him to take a steady shot, Brace found a way. He positioned himself at the end of the dugout bench and waited for the new Colorado Rockies and Florida Marlins to make their appearance. By now, Brace hardly needed to ask the players for permission to photograph them; usually, the players came to him.

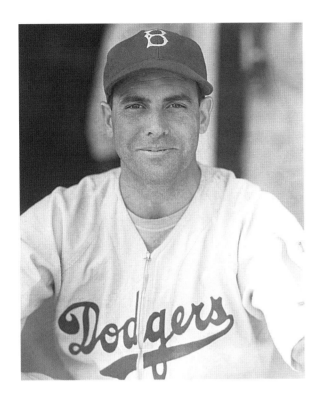 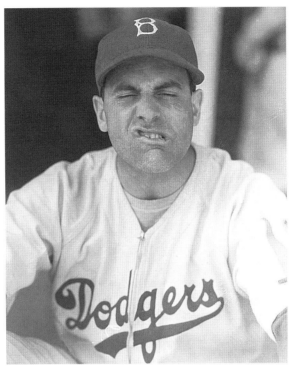

The next year, in 1994, eye problems forced Brace to call it quits behind the camera.

Brace's phone rings several times a week as former ballplayers call, looking for photos to help them recall their glory years. Ernie Banks has stopped by Brace's house. "I remember the cheers," Banks said, "but I don't remember what it looked like."

Those who are not ballplayers call as well. Baseball historians rely on his photos and his memory, autograph hunters order pictures so they can get them signed, and players' relatives call and write to fill gaps in family histories. A White Sox batboy asked for pictures of 1947: "I would like any remembrances of that year, which of course wasn't as special as it is now." Brace once received a letter from a woman requesting a photo of an obscure ballplayer from many years back. The woman explained that she'd had a one-night stand with the player and, unbeknownst to him, had borne his daughter. No attempt was ever made to contact the father, but the daughter did want to know what he looked like. Brace sent the picture.

Luke Sewell must have felt silly in a National League uniform. He was an American League catcher for 17 years before the Brooklyn Dodgers picked him up on waivers and then released him before he'd played a game.

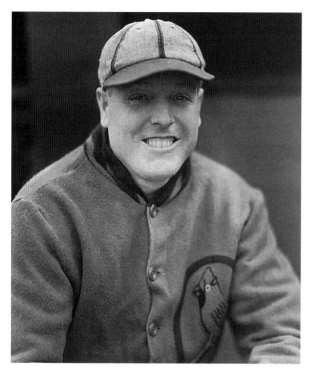

Si Johnson, who pitched from the 1920s through the 1940s before retiring and becoming a prison guard, was Brace's best customer. He ordered several thousand photos a year until his death in 1994.

BRACE MISSES THE EARLY YEARS. He misses Zeke Bonura's wild laugh and hard-drinking heroes such as Hack Wilson. He is left with memories, and negatives.

When did baseball start to change?

"I believe the game started to change after the war years," says Brace. "Players came back different. They didn't play as hard.

"Every one of the old timers died broke. They would tip us $10 for anything we did for them. Nowadays, if they've got a quarter coming back, they want it. I don't blame them; they never know what tomorrow will bring, they have no trade."

But in the old days, he repeats, the players played harder.

"If they got hurt, they wouldn't let you know about it. I remember Eddie Smith. He put an ice pick in his finger, but he wouldn't let them know about it. He went out and pitched. He said if he told them, they would put somebody else in there and he would be out of a job. Nowadays, they just get a little twinge in their finger and they say they can't play.

"It was all fun in them days. Now it is a regular business."

Brace is a modest man. He has never framed any of his photos. In fact, he seldom keeps any prints. Copies, he says, take up too much room. He has the negatives.

"Do you consider yourself an artist?" Brace is asked.

"No," he says.

"You don't think your pictures are art?"

"No. It's the camera. The camera is taking it. I just held the camera, that's all."

"Is it history?" he is asked.

"I suppose it is."

Lou Gehrig's favorite portrait. He ordered copies several times a year to autograph and send to fans.

Honus Wagner had long since retired as a shortstop when George Brace and George Burke photographed him as a coach at Wrigley Field. "He looked like the oldest person who ever played," Brace says. "It was hard to even imagine him as a player because he was so husky." Wagner finally left the game in 1951, 15 years after being elected to the Hall of Fame.

"There ain't much to being a ballplayer,
if you're a ballplayer."

—HONUS WAGNER

IMMORTALS

*Fifty men whose memories have endured—
some with a career of excellence, others
with a single season, a single game, or a
single moment of glory*

Two ingenious players from the 1890s became two of the preeminent managers of the twentieth century. Cornelius McGillicuddy, known as Connie Mack, led the Philadelphia Athletics for 50 years. Sitting as erect as a banker, Mack would move his team around the diamond by waving his scorecard from the dugout. John McGraw, who led the New York Giants for 29 years, had more of a win-at-all-costs attitude. In 1933, McGraw came out of retirement to lead the National League against Mack's American League in the first All-Star Game. McGraw never stepped onto a baseball field again.

As a manager, Casey Stengel could do no right in the National League and no wrong in the American League. His three National League teams never came close to the first division. His Yankees teams won 10 pennants and seven world championships from 1949 to 1960. But when the Yankees lost the 1960 World Series, the elderly Stengel was fired. Quoth Casey: "I'll never make the mistake of being 70 again."

Walter Johnson was the most feared pitcher of his time. Bob Feller and Nolan Ryan may have thrown the ball as fast, but nobody ever threw faster. Ray Chapman once took two strikes from Johnson and started walking back to the dugout. The umpire told him he had another one coming, and Chapman said, "Keep it. I don't want it." George Brace never saw Johnson play but photographed the Big Train as a manager.

Infielder Rogers Hornsby had the highest season batting average of the century but struck out as a manager. He was a perfectionist who wouldn't go to the movies and seldom read newspapers for fear he would weaken his batting eye. "His big problem was that he expected everyone to be as good as him," Brace says. "The players hated him."

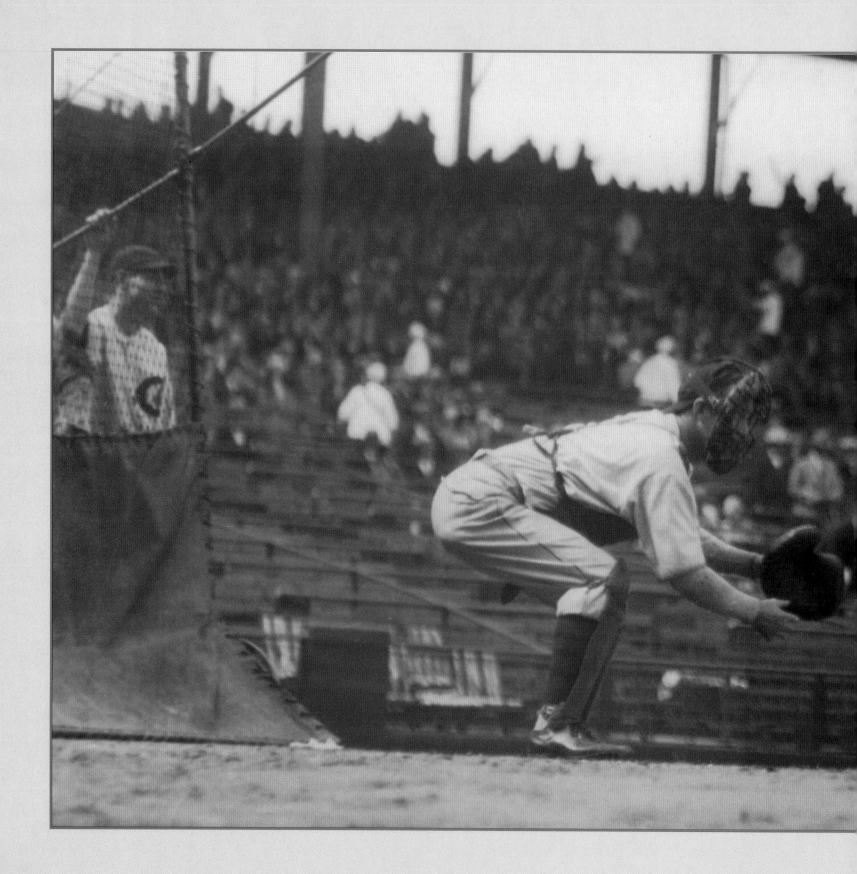

Hack Wilson was the closest thing the National League had to Babe Ruth when Burke and Brace started work. In 1930, Wilson drove in 190 runs, six more than any other player in modern baseball history. But Wilson hit the bottle as hard as he hit the baseball. "Ruth lasted longer because Hack got drunk too often," says Brace. "You could smell it on him." By 1935, Wilson was in the minors.

Frankie Frisch (below) had two great careers: one as John McGraw's hard-hitting, base-stealing second baseman with the Giants, and one as the fuel for the St. Louis Cardinals' Gashouse Gang. Each team made it to the World Series four times. Frisch, who never played a game in the minors, led the Cardinals to the world championship as a player-manager.

Charlie Gehringer (above) was "the Mechanical Man." Players said of him, "You wind him up in the spring, turn him loose, he hits .330 or .340, and you shut him off at the end of the season." The Tigers' second baseman, who could hit and field with uncommon grace, was more modest about his place in the universe. "Us ballplayers do things backward," he said. "First we play, then we retire and go to work."

Paul and Lloyd Waner—"Big Poison" and "Little Poison"—are the only modern-day brothers in the Hall of Fame. They roamed the outfield for the Pirates from the mid-1920s to 1940. "They were very close," says Brace, "and hung around together all the time." But they were complete opposites: Lloyd was a teetotaler and Paul was an alcoholic who brought whiskey to the park. "When I'm sober, the ball looks like an aspirin," Paul said. "When I'm drunk, the ball looks like a fuzzy grapefruit."

New York Giants pitcher Carl Hubbell, who won a record 26 games in a row over two seasons, had a strong fastball, an effective curve, and a devastating screwball. "The screwball's an unnatural pitch," said Hubbell. "Nature never intended a man to turn his hand like that throwing rocks at a bear."

Babe Ruth's home-run marks—60 in one season, 714 during his career—have been eclipsed, but their aura will shine forever. "He was the tops," says Brace. "Most old ballplayers in those days hit line drives. Ruth hit the ball a mile high. They floated out there." At Comiskey Park, Brace recalls, Ruth devoured both the pitching and the concessions: "He would send a batboy out to get him six or seven hot dogs in the middle of the game." Burke and Brace took more than 200 photographs of Ruth, most of them during his 15 years as a Yankee (left). Later, Ruth signed with the Boston Braves (below) but quit after 28 games. He returned three years later to coach the Dodgers (right).

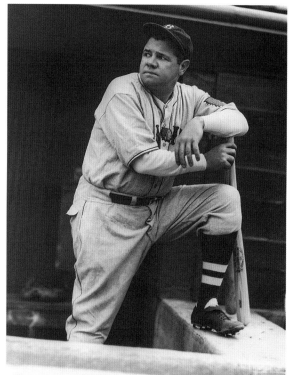

Catcher Bill Dickey was the bridge that connected the Yankees' Murderers Row of the 1920s to the Bronx Bombers of the 1930s. He caught at least 100 games a season for 13 consecutive years. Like Lou Gehrig, his roommate, Dickey was a quiet man. "He was just interested in baseball," says Brace. "He didn't talk to anybody. Even at Cooperstown, he hardly said a word." Dickey, the first player to be told of Gehrig's fatal illness, was the archetypal catcher who later appeared in the baseball films *The Pride of the Yankees* and *The Stratton Story*.

"There'll never be another like me," said pitcher Dizzy Dean, who became baseball's big draw after Babe Ruth's retirement. "Dean acted dumb, but I'm not sure if he really was," says Brace. In 1934, Dean was hit between the eyes by a thrown ball when he failed to slide into second base. "The doctors x-rayed my head and didn't find anything," he said. Dean, who switched equipment with a Latin American sportswriter named Ameriss for this picture, told different stories to reporters about his early life. "I was helpin' the writers out," he said. "Them ain't lies; them's scoops."

Lefty Grove won the American League earned-run-average title nine times, four more than anybody else. Overpowering and temperamental, Grove made life difficult for most people who covered baseball. Charles M. Conlon, the legendary baseball photographer, wrote that Grove consistently refused to pose for a shot of his grip. "Nobody has ever got that picture, and I guess nobody ever will," wrote Conlon in *The Sporting News* in 1937. "Lefty thinks this picture would reveal the secret of his skill." But Grove agreed to pose for Burke, his hunting buddy. "Lefty would do anything for us," Brace says.

Mel Ott was the nice guy in Leo Durocher's "nice guys finish last" quote. He led the Giants in home runs for 18 years, from 1928 to 1945. Brace sent Ott a set of photos from his playing days in 1958, just days before he was killed in an auto accident. This photo was not included. Brace, who took the picture in the Giants' dugout, never even printed the photo until the mid-1990s.

Al Simmons and his wife, Doris, show off their new Hupmobile outside Comiskey Park. Simmons, born Aloysius Harry Szymanski, lived with his mother in Milwaukee before his marriage in 1934. He was known as "Bucketfoot Al" because of his odd, wide stance. Connie Mack labeled Simmons the greatest hitter he ever managed. Said Mack: "I don't care if he stands on his head so long as he keeps murdering the ball."

Bill Terry (below) was the National League's last .400 hitter. He retired as a player in 1936 with one of the highest lifetime averages in major league history, but it took 18 years before he reached the Hall of Fame. Terry, who succeeded John McGraw as Giants manager, was surly: to sportswriters, to fans, even to George Brace, who had trouble talking to him at Cooperstown years after his retirement. "He wouldn't talk to anybody," Brace says.

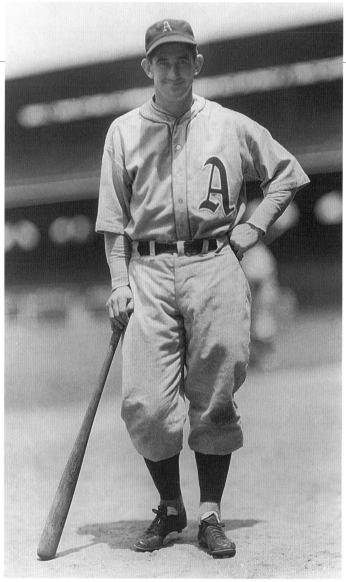

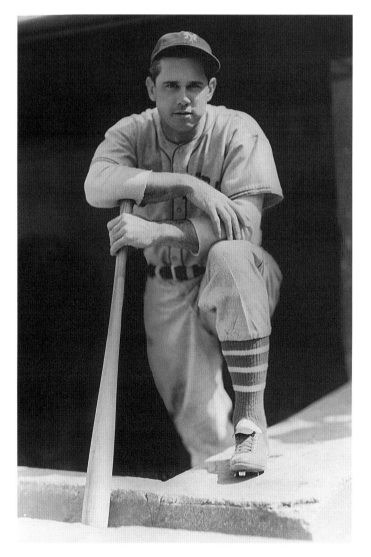

Mickey Cochrane (above) had a frightening end to his playing career on May 25, 1937, when he was hit in the head by a fastball thrown by Bump Hadley. Doctors gave him a 50-50 chance of surviving as he was wheeled into surgery. When he recovered, Cochrane wanted to play again but was prevented from doing so by Tigers owner Walter Briggs. Cochrane, who retired with the highest lifetime batting average for catchers, came back to manage.

Jimmie Foxx, held in a headlock by wrestler Ed "Strangler" Lewis, was one of the strongest hitters in baseball history. "He has muscles in his hair," said pitcher Lefty Gomez of his nemesis. "The Beast," Foxx's nickname, fit his batting style but not his personality. "He was a murderous hitter but too nice for his own good," says Brace. "He would tip us, and everybody else." Foxx ended up managing a women's baseball team. He died nearly broke.

Lou Gehrig was Brace's favorite player. "He was a quiet man. He never volunteered anything," Brace says. "But if you approached him, he would talk for hours." Brace photographed Gehrig in 1934 with children who had won a national contest sponsored by a creamery. Brace's collection includes a dozen other photographs showing the kindness Gehrig exhibited toward each child. Melvin Wild (right photo) was 10 when his picture was taken. Wild cherished the print and showed it to the Orioles' Cal Ripken in 1995, just weeks before Ripken broke Gehrig's Iron Man record. Then Wild had his picture taken with another Iron Man.

Gabby Hartnett was always laughing, always smiling, always talking, says Brace—which is why he was called Gabby. Brace was on the field when the strapping Cubs catcher slammed his "Homer in the Gloamin'" to help the Cubs clinch the National League pennant in 1938. Brace and other photographers followed Hartnett down the third-base line into a mob of well-wishers at home plate.

Hank Greenberg came close to breaking Babe Ruth's single-season home-run total in 1938. With five days to go, Greenberg needed only two homers to tie Ruth's mark. Greenberg's mother promised to cook 61 portions of gefilte fish in the shape of baseballs if he beat Ruth's record, but the fish never flew. After four years in the army, Greenberg returned to the Tigers in 1945, hitting a homer on his first day back with a team that went on to win the world championship.

Joe Cronin was the ultimate baseball man. He started as a substitute second baseman for the Pittsburgh Pirates in 1926, worked his way up to All-Star shortstop for the Washington Senators and Boston Red Sox, and managed the Red Sox to the World Series in 1946. After his playing days, Cronin served two terms as president of the American League, where he oversaw the league's first expansion and introduced the designated hitter rule.

When Bob Feller was a 17-year-old in Van Meter, Iowa, he signed a Cleveland Indians contract for a modest bonus: two autographed baseballs and a scorecard from the 1935 All-Star Game. Feller became the game's greatest prodigy, striking out 15 batters in his first major league start. His magic continued for 18 seasons, which saw him pitch 3 no-hitters and 12 one-hitters. Feller was considered egotistical by many. Brace disagrees: "People thought he was stuck up, but he had a twitch in his eye and he would always look away. The impression people had of Feller never left."

"If there was ever a man born to be a hitter, it was me," said Ted Williams, who came to the Red Sox outfield at age 20 after a year with the minor league Minneapolis Millers. Fans used to show up for batting practice just to watch Williams's casual, easy swing send balls into the upper deck. "He was the best hitter of all time," says Brace. "He would have had close to 800 homers had he not donated five years of his life to the service." Brace learned not to talk to the Splendid Splinter near the batting cage. "When he held a bat in his hand, he was concentrating 100 percent on hitting. That's when a lot of sportswriters got in trouble."

Kenesaw Mountain Landis, the man
credited with bringing baseball back
to respectability following the 1919
Black Sox scandal, was a backroom
boss who was generally disliked by
both players and owners. Landis was
a tyrant who kept blacks out of
baseball. He worked out of Chicago
and was a frequent visitor to Wrigley
Field. "We saw him there all the
time," says Brace. "He was always
quite willing to pose."

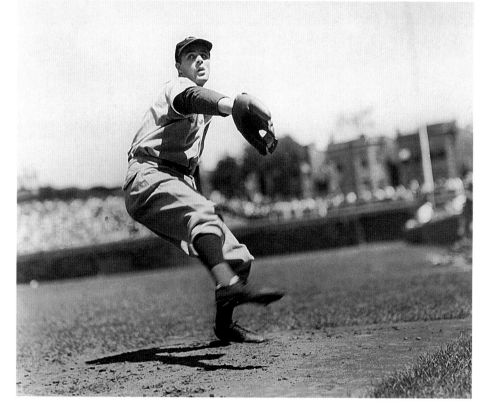

Johnny Vander Meer pitched back-
to-back no-hitters in June 1938, a
feat as remarkable as Joe DiMaggio's
56-game hitting streak. Unlike
DiMaggio, however, Vander Meer's
performance was part of an otherwise
mediocre career. The games came
early in his first full season, so great
things were expected of the Reds
lefty. But Vander Meer never won 20
games in any season and ended up
losing more games than he won. He
never complained about pitching for
subpar teams, Brace says. "The two
games never went to his head."

Lou Boudreau (below), baseball's boy wonder, took over as Cleveland's player-manager at age 24 and eventually led his team to a world championship. Bad ankles limited his range at shortstop and kept him out of the military, but Boudreau learned to position himself against hitters, making him one of the best infielders of his era. In 1951, Brace sent telegrams to top baseball officials informing them of George Burke's death. Boudreau was the only one to respond.

Pete Gray (above) became a symbol of the game during the war years. After losing his right arm in a boyhood accident, he learned to throw and hit from the left side, earning a shot in the majors after hitting .333 with the Memphis Chicks in 1944. But he hit only .218 in 61 games with the St. Louis Browns during the 1945 season. Brace, an army medic in the Pacific at the time, never saw Gray play. Burke told Brace's replacement not to show Gray's empty right sleeve, but the view was difficult to avoid.

Yogi Berra, one of baseball's greatest
catchers and one of the game's best
bad-ball hitters, may be remembered
longest for his Yogi-isms. Once, Berra
struck out swinging on three pitches
well out of the strike zone and then
returned to the dugout wondering,
"How can a pitcher that wild be in
the big leagues?" Silly? Profound?
Brace was never quite sure. "He did
say these things," Brace recalls, "but
we were never quite sure just what
they meant, and I'm not sure he
knew either."

Joe DiMaggio led the Yankees to the World Series 10 times during his 13-year career. In 1941, the year Ted Williams batted .406, DiMaggio's 56-game hitting streak helped him win the league's Most Valuable Player Award. Always fighting injuries, DiMaggio had a toughness that matched his talent. "When he started to fade, he decided to get out before it was too late," says Brace. Following his retirement, DiMaggio was asked about his upcoming marriage to Marilyn Monroe. Replied the Yankee Clipper: "It's got to be better than rooming with Joe Page."

Leo Durocher (shown with a young fan) was the ultimate lifer. During his 17-year career as a shortstop, Durocher never hit close to .300. But he was a utility man for the Yankees, captain of the Gashouse Gang, and an All-Star three times. As a manager, Leo the Lip specialized in turning average players into overachievers. His teams won three pennants, including one world championship. Hated and loved, Durocher led the National League in baiting umpires, womanizing, hanging out with Hollywood stars, and playing gin rummy.

"I was there when Jackie Robinson first came up," says Brace. "It was a big deal. Players refused to associate with him and he faced a great deal of pressure." According to Brace, Robinson brought a whole new way to play the game, a reckless, exciting brand of baseball with aggressive baserunning. "He had to be cocky to survive, but he was not as great a player as they say," Brace recalls. "He didn't last long and there were players better than him."

Roy Campanella (below), spark plug of Brooklyn's Boys of Summer, led the Dodgers to five pennants and won three Most Valuable Player Awards. His playing days ended in 1958, when he lost control of his car on an icy street and crashed into a telephone pole. Campy was paralyzed and lived the rest of his life as a quadriplegic. His smile, strength, and warmth never dimmed, says Brace.

Satchel Paige (above) was the greatest pitcher who ever lived, according to Dizzy Dean, Charlie Gehringer, and Joe DiMaggio. But his best years were well behind him by the time he became the American League's first black pitcher. Paige pitched in the Negro Leagues from the 1920s through the 1940s and made his mark as a barnstormer. He beat Dean in four of six exhibition games in 1934, when Dean was at the top of his form. Brace says Paige was polite but quiet after joining the Indians in 1947. "The fact that most baseball fans didn't see him in his prime is one of the great tragedies of the game," says Brace.

Willie Mays was the most exciting player of his generation. He combined power and speed with sublime fielding, making many of the game's greatest catches. "I don't compare 'em. I just catch 'em," he once said. Mays seemed equally at home playing stickball on the streets of Harlem and catching fly balls in the huge expanse of the Polo Grounds. Although he starred for the Giants in the team's first 14 years on the West Coast, he always looked best in a New York uniform.

"The Duke of Flatbush," Duke Snider, had more home runs and RBI during the 1950s than any other player. He posted better statistics than New York's other great center fielders, Willie Mays of the Giants and Mickey Mantle of the Yankees, in the four seasons their careers overlapped. He developed into a great center fielder with good range and a good arm, but he may be best remembered for what this picture hardly hints at—his prematurely gray hair.

"Here stands baseball's happy warrior; here stands baseball's perfect knight," said baseball commissioner Ford Frick when Stan Musial's statue was dedicated outside St. Louis's Busch Stadium. Musial, as personable as he was talented, was the most difficult out in the National League during the 1940s and 1950s. Preacher Roe's pitching advice against Musial was sage. "I throw four wide ones, and then I try to pick him off."

"Maybe I'm not a great man, but I damn well want to break the record," said Roger Maris during that fateful 1961 season as he chased and caught the ghost of Babe Ruth. His mark of 61 home runs has stood as long as Ruth's mark of 60. Maris was an excellent fielder and a dangerous hitter who had many good years before and after his record-breaking season. Brace, who first took note of Maris as a young Kansas City outfielder, says, "He was the most underrated player I ever saw."

"All I have is natural ability," said Mickey Mantle. What sounds like a boast was really a curse for the Yankee star who excelled in all aspects of the game and from both sides of the plate. Mantle, named after catcher Mickey Cochrane, was constantly dogged by injury and pain. Taking over for Joe DiMaggio in center field, he led the Yankees to 12 American League pennants and seven World Series rings. Mantle could hit the ball farther than anybody but the Babe. "If he'd stayed healthy, he could have been the best ever," says Brace.

The Pirates' Harvey Haddix (below) pitched the longest perfect game in baseball history. On May 26, 1959, he completed 12 flawless innings against the Milwaukee Braves, which boasted a lineup that included Hank Aaron, Eddie Mathews, and Joe Adcock. It was Adcock who finally drove in the run to make Haddix an unlikely loser.

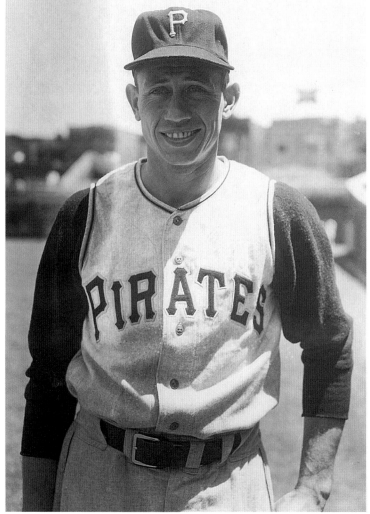

Don Larsen (above) will be remembered for pitching his perfect game in the 1956 World Series. "He did it with a tremendous assortment of pitches that seemed to have five forward speeds, including a slow one that ought to have been equipped with backup lights," wrote Shirley Povich, of the *Washington Post*. Larsen posed often for Brace because the pitcher appeared on nine teams during his 14-year career. Although the pitcher ended with a losing record, he had his day in the sun.

One swing of the bat made Bobby Thomson immortal. Thomson's ninth-inning homer to end the one-game National League playoff was the miracle that propelled the Giants over the mighty Brooklyn Dodgers in 1951. Thomson's career was not distinguished—he batted .270—but he was named a starter, along with Mel Ott and Willie Mays, in the New York Giants' all-time outfield. The Dodgers' Ralph Branca, who wore number 13 and had won 13 games when his pitch became the "Shot Heard 'Round the World," changed his number after that season.

Hank Aaron sneaked up on baseball fans. "No doubt he was a good hitter and a good fielder, but nobody realized how great he was until the end," says Brace. The end was 755 home runs, 41 more than Babe Ruth. Aaron, along with Ernie Banks, brought a new power swing to baseball, using quick wrists rather than brute strength to drive baseballs out of the park. Aaron, who never hit 50 home runs in any season, admitted: "If I had to pay to go see somebody play for one game, I wouldn't pay to see Hank Aaron. I wasn't flashy. I didn't start fights. I didn't rush out to the mound every time a pitch came near me. I didn't hustle after fly balls that were 20 rows back in the seats. But if I had to pay to see someone play in a three-game series, I'd rather see myself."

On his first day at Wrigley Field, near the end of the 1953 season, Ernie Banks posed for Brace. Shy and slight, Banks gave no hint of the homers hidden in his swing. He was one of the kindest players Brace ever encountered. "Usually players will talk to kids for a second, but Banks—and Nellie Fox—introduced kids to everyone in the clubhouse." Said longtime White Sox manager Jimmy Dykes: "Without Ernie Banks, the Cubs would finish in Albuquerque."

Whitey Ford (below) retired from baseball with one of the highest winning percentages ever. "The Chairman of the Board" led the Yankees not with overpowering pitches, but with the ability to pitch just a little better than his opponents. He threw 33 consecutive shutout World Series innings and won more Series games than any pitcher.

Sandy Koufax (above), the youngest player elected to the Hall of Fame, put together six of the greatest years in pitching. Arm troubles forced him to retire in 1966 after compiling a 27–9 record in his final season. "I know Koufax's weakness," said Whitey Ford. "He can't hit."

"I want to be remembered as a ballplayer who gave all he had to give," said Roberto Clemente. Brace says Clemente was the best all-around player he ever saw. He won four National League batting titles, had the game's best outfield arm, and always seemed to know just what to do with the ball. Brace says that Clemente, a Puerto Rican, was uncomfortable speaking English during his first years in the majors. But he became a role model before his death in a 1972 plane crash while on a mercy mission for Nicaraguan earthquake survivors. Said baseball commissioner Bowie Kuhn: "He had about him a touch of royalty."

"A hot dog at the ballpark is better
than steak at the Ritz."

—HUMPHREY BOGART

GRANDSTANDS

The game wasn't confined to the field for Burke and Brace—

it was a pageant that included the fans, batboys, trainers,

and concessionaires.

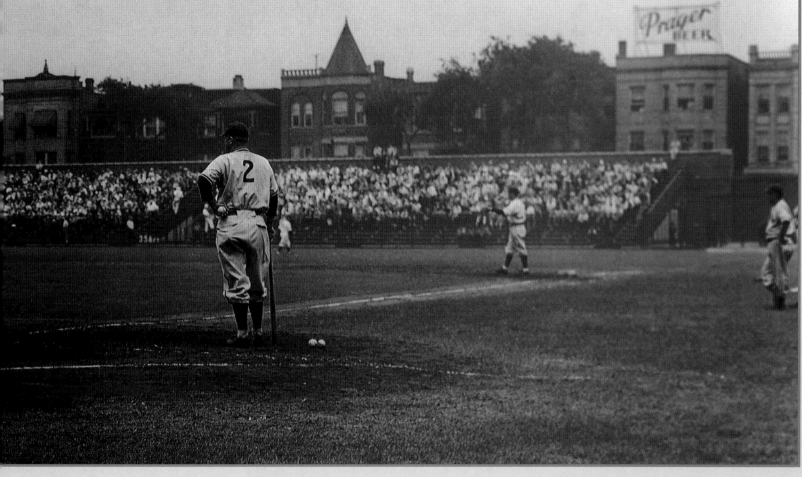

Players take warm-ups at Wrigley
Field on Opening Day in 1932, when
the old scoreboard featured the
Wrigley's gum "stick men."

All roads lead to Wrigley Field: the elevated train station at Broadway and Lawrence and the front entrance to the park at Clark and Addison, the Cubs' home since 1916.

There was no such thing as a sellout crowd at Wrigley Field during the early '30s. When all the seats were filled, fans could sit on the field and along the outfield fences; any ball bouncing into the crowd was a ground-rule double.

July 1937: Workers begin renovating Wrigley Field, dismantling the outfield seats and the old scoreboard in preparation for the construction of the current bleachers and scoreboard. Cubs executive Bill Veeck Jr. hired George Brace to visit the park every day or two to document the progress.

Working high and low: the construction of the main ramp in the bleacher section.

Wooden seats are built into the steel frame of the new bleachers. Work continued even during the games. Once, a construction worker was beaned by a home run.

While one crew works high above the surrounding neighborhood, another installs a new tradition: ivy on the outfield's brick wall.

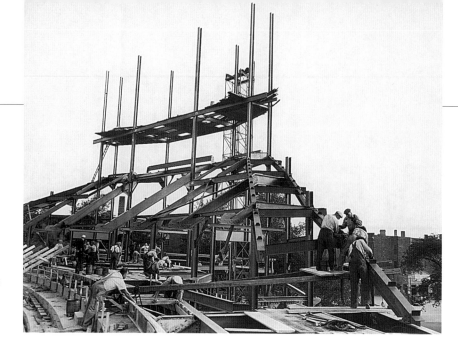

Running up the scoreboard. At the time, it was a state-of-the-art marvel; today, it's a charming relic.

Sandbags were stacked in the newly built seats to ensure that they could support the weight of fans who would soon occupy them. As an added touch, Veeck tried to get Chinese elm trees to grow beside the scoreboard, but the idea never took root. Possible causes of death: small planters, rough treatment from fans, and the brutal winds off nearby Lake Michigan.

A stadium that endures. Even today, says Brace, "It's still a modern park."

Comiskey Park, at 35th Street and Shields Avenue on Chicago's South Side, was called the "Baseball Palace of the World" when it opened in 1910. The park was designed by Zachary Taylor Davis, the same architect who later designed Wrigley Field. It was the oldest stadium in baseball when it was torn down in 1991.

August 14, 1939: the first night game at Comiskey.

Comiskey Park as it looked years before Bill Veeck Jr. bought the club and installed his "exploding" scoreboard in dead center field. Number 38 at left is White Sox bullpen coach Muddy Ruel.

Retired bricklayer Harry Thobe was the Cincinnati Red Rooter, making a guest appearance at the 1938 World Series at Wrigley Field.

Fan Joanne Lubin was a regular at both Wrigley and Comiskey during the 1950s.

Baseball's first Ladies Day was held at Wrigley Field, and it was a popular feature for years. Wrigley's record crowd was 51,556 on June 27, 1930—a Ladies Day.

Before ballplayers slipped out the back door: Cubs pitcher Clay Bryant signs autographs near the steps leading to the clubhouse.

Fillies and Phillies: Beauty queens pose with Glen Gorbous and Ron Negray in the right-field corner at Wrigley Field for a 1955 promotion.

Clarence Wadley, a jewelry craftsman from Chicago's South Side, had plenty of big league customers for his bracelet charms with etched team logos and inset diamonds. Here he takes orders from the Cardinals' Dizzy Dean and Pepper Martin.

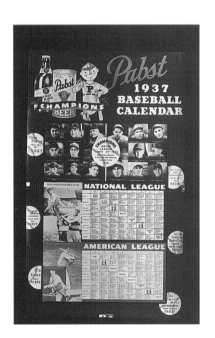

Beer was on the calendar, popcorn was a production, and the concession ladies stood ready to serve.

A cigarette seller at Wrigley Field. Brace didn't know her name and identified her as "the Ciggy Girl" in his photo file.

George Brace documented two big events in the concession business during the late 1930s: the introduction of a new "smoky links" cart at Wrigley Field and canned beer at Comiskey Park. Major league ballparks went back to glass bottles when World War II increased the demand for tin.

Wrigley ticket manager George Doyle (right) and an assistant field the phones as they trim their ticket trees.

"Hot dog gals" Mildred and Eleanor.

The army of ushers at Comiskey.

Whenever someone asked usher Joe Murphy to estimate the attendance at Wrigley or Comiskey, he would say, "40,000." So he became known as "40,000 Murphy."

Bandmaster Jack Bramhall and his musicians played the base notes at Wrigley Field.

S. E. Watters started out as a biology teacher but ended up dissecting the business of baseball as traveling secretary for the Pittsburgh Pirates.

They were "clubhouse boys" for decades at Comiskey Park. They were brothers and they shared the same nickname, "Sharkey." Their real names were Art and Ephraim Colledge, but it hardly mattered, says Brace: "No one ever called them anything but Sharkey."

The "field men" at Wrigley guard their turf. In the suit is head groundskeeper Bobby Dorr, whose apartment was actually inside Wrigley Field. He lived in a single-family home built under the seats in the left-field corner.

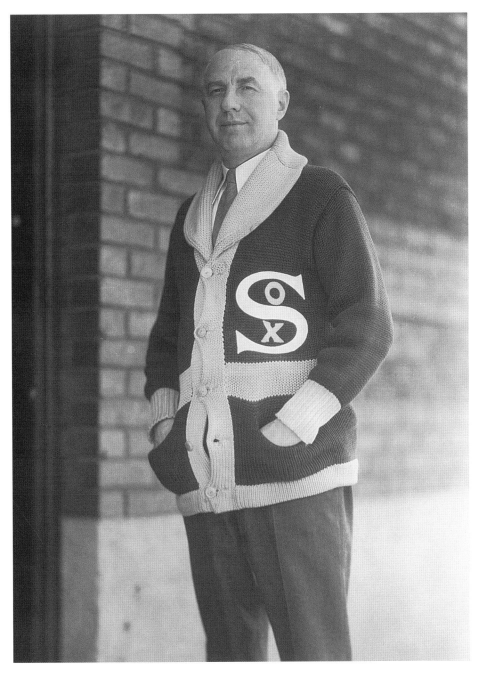

William Dwyre paints the foul line—and his pants—at Wrigley Field.

Team sweaters were already falling out of fashion when groundskeeper Henry Chamberlain modeled this one at Comiskey Park around 1930.

Paul Dominick was a popular mascot for the Cubs in the 1930s. Here he clowns around with Rabbit Maranville, stages a fake fight with Sox batboy Mickey Maguire, and tries to catch some attention all by himself. Later, Dominick went to Hollywood, where he joined the "Our Gang" cast.

Batboy Paul Wick lines up the
Milwaukee Braves' hatchets.

Wʜɪᴛᴇ Sox batboy Pat Lyons with a certain well-known player on the opposing team.

Steve Basil started out as a minor league catcher and worked as a movie projectionist before sliding safely into a career as an American League umpire.

The last decision of Babe Pinelli's career was the called strike three against Dale Mitchell in Don Larsen's World Series perfect game.

When Lon Warneke retired as a player, he took up umpiring. It was a hard job because he had to steer clear of his ballplaying friends. He ended up as a county judge in his native Arkansas.

Charles Moran, George Magerkurth, and George Parker at Wrigley Field. A fan once ran out of the stands and assaulted Magerkurth at home plate; Magerkurth was the aggressor in several other off-the-field fistfights with players and fans.

Bob Elson, interviewing Zeke Bonura, did the play-by-play for the White Sox for 40 years. Whenever a Sox player hit a home run, Elson would declare it a "White Owl wallop." It was no coincidence that White Owl cigars sponsored his show.

WLS Radio in Chicago was the first station to offer daily broadcasts of major league games. Hal Totten, who called games for both the Cubs and Sox, is shown with assistant John Larsen and Cubs Charlie Grimm, Woody English, and Lon Warneke. Totten was the first broadcaster to hold on-the-field interviews.

W<small>CFL</small>'s Bob Hawk poses at Wrigley Field with waitresses from Ricketts, a restaurant down the street from the ballpark. Hawk later became a national radio quizmaster, the first to ask "the $64 question," an early version of "The $64,000 Question."

H<small>arry</small> Caray started his long baseball career as an announcer for the St. Louis Cardinals in 1945. His rendition of "Take Me Out to the Ballgame" became a drawing card as he worked for the Oakland Athletics, White Sox, and Cubs during a career spanning more than 50 years.

When Cubs trainer Andy Lotshaw ran out of liniment one day, he rubbed Coca-Cola on pitcher Guy Bush's arm. Bush liked the effect, and Lotshaw used Coca-Cola on Bush from that time on.

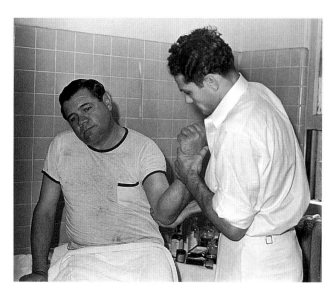

Dodgers trainer Ed Froelich works on the left arm of coach Babe Ruth. Froelich, who began his baseball career as a Cubs batboy in 1926, worked as a trainer for the Dodgers, Yankees, Red Sox, and White Sox before quitting in 1967 to become a salesman in the corrugated container business.

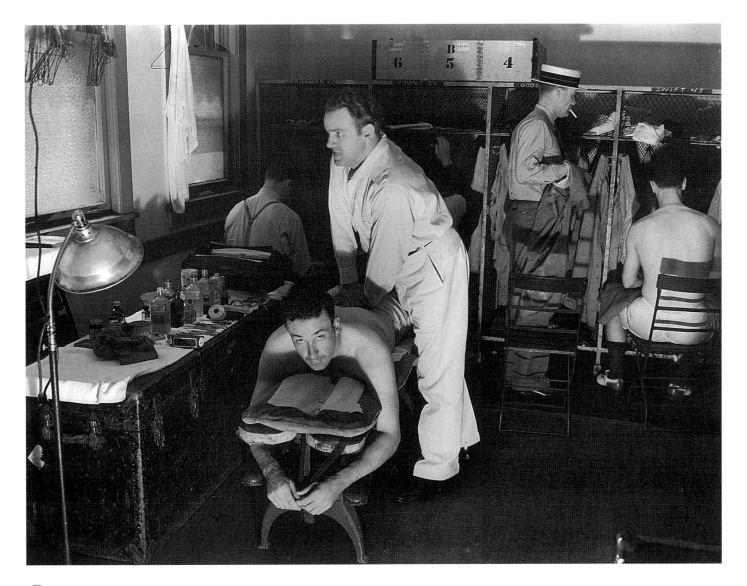

Charles A. Jorgenson, Pirates trainer for 29 years, rubs down outfielder Johnny Rizzo in the visiting locker room at Wrigley in 1938. In the background: shortstop Arky Vaughan, coach Johnny Gooch, and pitcher Bill Swift.

Comiskey's visiting clubhouse is empty while the Sox are on deck, playing cards before the game. At the table: Les Tietje, Luke Sewell, batting practice pitcher Tommy Stevens, clubhouse boy Art "Sharkey" Colledge, and Clint Brown.

Call the game, already! Sox players have changed into their street clothes while awaiting the umpire's official word on canceling a rained-out game. Those clearly visible are Thornton Lee, Ted Lyons (with cigar), Tony Rensa, Mike Kreevich, and Henry Steinbacher.

You can run into some interesting people when you work security at the ballparks. Guard Jerry Alicoate with Mickey Mantle, Willie Mays, Nellie Fox, Roger Maris, and Stan Musial.

Men in white hats: Cubs coach Mike Kelley joins players Woody English, Chuck Klein, Riggs Stephenson, Gabby Hartnett, Kiki Cuyler, Lon Warneke, Charlie Root, and Babe Herman on a shopping trip to Herbert's Men's Store in 1934. According to a team tradition, the first victory in September called for players to destroy their straw hats and replace them with felt fedoras.

"Baseball players are the
weirdest of all. I think it's
all that organ music."

—WRITER PETER GENT

PLAYING AROUND

*The players were competitors during the game and
clowns and carousers before and after. And they
were friends with Burke and Brace, who captured
their unguarded moments in photographs.*

Chewing up the league: Billy Herman, Guy Bush, Bob Smith, Zack Taylor, Woody English, and Charlie Root.

Manager Charlie "Jolly Cholly" Grimm had to deal with several Cubs on the bottle, including this baby bear brought to Wrigley Field.

Posing for Burke and Brace was pure fun for most ballplayers. New York Giants outfielders Jim Ripple and Mel Ott tipped their caps for the camera.

The Cubs' Billy Jurges and Kiki Cuyler showed that their team was not all business in the 1930s, despite winning three pennants.

Pepper Martin, who played accordion and outfield, was the leader of the Mudcat Band, which helped the Cardinals' Gashouse Gang tune up in the 1930s. On guitar: Lon Warneke and Bill McGee. In the background: Dick Siebert, Ray Harrell, Herb Bremer, and Jimmy Brown.

Orlando Cepeda compares a small, vintage 1930s-era first baseman's glove with his own glove around 1959.

Fans introduce Sox infielder Don "Cab" Kolloway to a puppet made in his likeness.

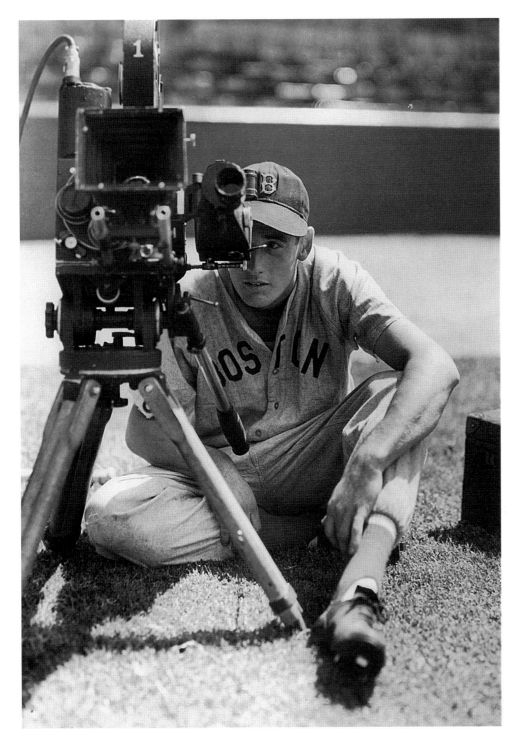

During a visit to Comiskey Park, Ted Williams focuses a movie camera on George Brace. Williams was constantly feuding with the news media, but "he was always friendly to Mr. Burke and me," says Brace. Williams's father was a photographer.

Al Schacht was a Washington Senators pitcher and coach before becoming a full-time clown. Schacht said that once, as a pitcher, he walked the first batter and said, "There goes my perfect game." The next batter singled and he said, "There goes my no-hitter." Schacht gave up a double to the next hitter and said, "There goes my shutout." And when the fourth batter homered, he said, "There goes Schacht."

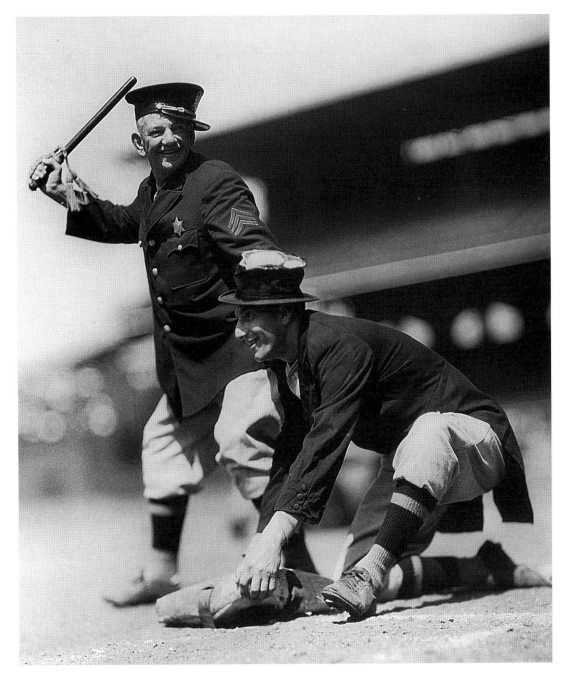

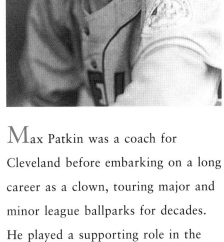

Max Patkin was a coach for Cleveland before embarking on a long career as a clown, touring major and minor league ballparks for decades. He played a supporting role in the film *Bull Durham*.

Schacht attempts to steal a base but is caught by Nick Altrock, another former player who became a baseball clown.

In the 1930s, Cubs fans would gather at Chicago's Dearborn Street train station every February to give the team a big, band-filled send-off to spring training. Gabby Hartnett signs autographs and bids adieu before the team's trek to Catalina Island, off California.

The White Sox held Ted Lyons Day
in 1940 to honor their popular
veteran. Lyons, who was with the Sox
from 1923 to 1946, had become a
"Sunday pitcher," appearing only
once a week to conserve his aging
arm and attract big weekend crowds.
Lyons found that ironic: "When I was
a kid, my mother wouldn't let me
play ball on Sunday." On his special
day, he let Brace follow him around,
from private shave to public wave.

The Cubs sent manager Joe McCarthy packing at the end of the 1930 season, and when he returned to Chicago with the Yankees, his admirers presented him with luggage at Comiskey Park. McCarthy, the most successful manager in baseball history, crosses his arms as players and officials join him in a tribute. The rotund man to his left is Alderman Joe McDonough. The Yankee coach to his right is Jimmy Burke.

Road trips: Frank Grube, Monty Stratton, Italo Chelini, Mike Kreevich, Vern Kennedy, and Clint Brown line up beside a White Sox trailer, while Luke Appling, Tom Turner, and Thornton Lee stand by their Chryslers.

Cubs outfielder Augie Galan with his shiny new Lincoln Zephyr in the Wrigley Field parking lot.

Infielder Francis "Salty" Parker was in the right place at the right time. On Parker's first day in the big leagues in 1936, Detroit's general manager invited all the Tigers to a banquet. Parker and five veterans accepted, and the executive surprised all six by presenting them with new Chevys. Parker lasted only 11 games in the majors, but at least he had something to drive away in.

Actors Charles Correll and Freeman Gosden, who played Amos and Andy on the radio show of the same name, try out for the Cubs during a stop at Wrigley Field.

Actress and dancer Lupe Velez, "the Mexican Spitfire" who married and divorced *Tarzan* star Johnny Weissmuller, gets tips from Cubs Joe Marty and Stan Hack.

New York City Mayor Fiorello LaGuardia made sure to get his picture taken with Joe DiMaggio and Lou Gehrig at the 1938 World Series.

Singing cowboy Gene Autry got off of his horse long enough to visit Cub pitcher Guy Bush. Autry, who serenaded Cubs players in the locker room, later became owner of the California Angels.

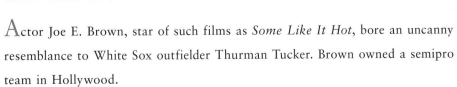

Actor Joe E. Brown, star of such films as *Some Like It Hot*, bore an uncanny resemblance to White Sox outfielder Thurman Tucker. Brown owned a semipro team in Hollywood.

Charlie Root, the Cubs pitcher who gave up Babe Ruth's legendary "Called Shot," traded his baseball cap for a 10-gallon hat and a Shriner's fez during a visit to George Burke's photo studio.

Lon Warneke goes western in Burke's studio. "Lon had just bought a farm with cattle, so when he saw the cowboy outfit, he put it on for fun," recalled Warneke's wife, Charlyne.

One of the most unusual aspects of Brace's collection shows baseball players in civilian clothes. Burke and Brace were encouraged to take photographs of players out of uniform for *Who's Who in the Major Leagues*. Dozens stopped by the studio. Others, including stars from as far back as the turn of the century, paused at the ballpark for their portraits.

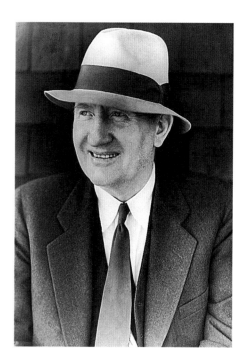

Joe Tinker: The shortstop in "Tinker to Evers to Chance," he brought defense and four World Series to the early Cubs.

Mordecai "Three-Finger" Brown: When he was a boy, his pitching hand was mangled in a farm accident. When he was a man, that mangled hand put extra spin on the ball.

Clarence "Dazzy" Vance: He pitched his first victory at age 31 and went on to win nearly 200 more with the Dodgers.

Sox pitcher John Rigney with Mickey the barber.

Paul Richards: A utility catcher in the 1930s and '40s, he became one of the game's most respected general managers.

Jimmy Dykes finished in first and last place several times during his 44 years in baseball. "When you're winning," he said, "beer tastes better."

The arms dealer: White Sox trainer Ad Schacht (top) with two of his clients—pitchers Ted Lyons and George Earnshaw.

George Sisler's great hitting career was cut short by sinusitis that damaged his batting eye.

Tris Speaker, a star of the 1920s, was just another fan in the stands in the 1930s.

Muddy Ruel: He was the catcher on the day Carl Mays's pitch struck and killed batter Ray Chapman in 1920.

Hazen "Kiki" Cuyler's nickname was not pronounced "Kee-Kee." Instead it sounded like "Kuy-Kuy" and came from other outfielders shortening his last name as they signaled for him to take fly balls: "Cuy! Cuy!"

Chuck Dressen: As a manager, he was known for telling his players, "Hold 'em, boys. I'll think of something." Most often he did.

Dolph Camilli: A leader of the Brooklyn Dodgers, he refused to report to the Giants when traded.

Fred Lindstrom: At age 18, he starred in the 1924 World Series, banging out four hits in one game against Walter Johnson.

Detroit Tigers pitcher Paul Trout looks so distinguished, you'd never think his nickname was "Dizzy."

Many ballplayers joined the military, giving up prime years in their careers, when America went to war in 1941. Below: Navy men John Rigney and Bob Feller played at various times for the baseball team at Great Lakes Naval Training Center north of Chicago. Right photos: Mickey Cochrane, naval officer and Great Lakes manager, lost more than major league baseball during the war: his son died in the service.

Gabby Hartnett holds a trophy won by his amateur baseball team in 1938.

The Israelite House of David, a religious group based in Benton Harbor, Michigan, formed a barnstorming baseball team that played against major league, minor league, and Negro League teams. All members of the sect wore beards, including second baseman Joe Franz, pictured here with his sisters.

Hack Wilson, described as a "high-ball hitter on the field and off," was available for autographs at this Chicago bar.

Ray Schalk caught four no-hitters during his 1912–1929 career, and in the 40 years that followed, he sent a telegram of congratulations to every catcher who caught a no-hitter. Because Schalk knew all about strikes, it was natural for him to own a bowling alley in Chicago, where he was assisted by snack bar worker June Lutrick.

Lou Gehrig relaxes in the lobby of the Del Prado Hotel on Chicago's South Side, where he met his beloved wife, Eleanor.

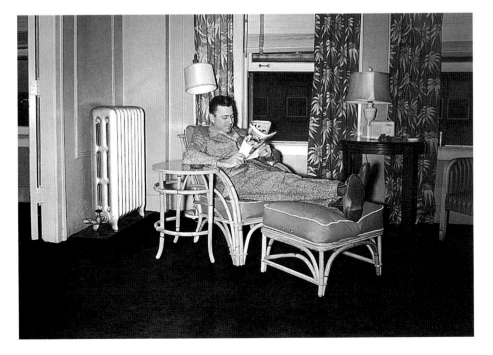

William Jennings Bryan Herman was more casual than his name might indicate. The Hall of Fame second baseman was known as Billy.

Rifle-armed Cubs third baseman Stan Hack cleans a gun in his living room. He was an avid duck hunter.

The Cubs' Ripper Collins suffered a season-ending injury when he slid into home in August 1937. But even a broken ankle and a trip to the hospital couldn't wipe the smile off the face of the fun-loving first baseman.

Cubs star Phil Cavarretta's Chicago home was a gathering place for neighborhood kids (he's sitting in short center field in the midst of the mob).

Cavarretta steps up to the plates in the kitchen of his home.

The Babe and the babe: Ruth with his second wife, Claire, a former New York model.

*"We're not going on a honeymoon.
We're going to go to work and
win another pennant."*

—CLAIRE RUTH, AFTER HER WEDDING IN 1929

HOME TEAMS

*Players often asked Burke and Brace to
take pictures of them with their wives
and children, and the photographers
were happy to comply, assembling a
family album of baseball.*

Husbands and Wives

Yankees pitcher Vernon "Lefty" Gomez and musical comedy star June O'Dea had a marriage full of great fun and terrible fights. At their divorce hearing, June told the judge of Lefty's threat to murder her: "He could do it, he said, because everyone thought he loved me. He said he would wear gloves and choke me to death and leave. He would come back later, he said, and discover me and tell everybody his wife had been killed." Amazingly, the pair reconciled.

Philadelphia A's owner Connie Mack and his wife, Katharine, at the 1938 World Series. Seven years later, the couple split up in a family dispute over who would own the team. The 83-year-old Mack was distraught: "In the 35 years Mrs. McGillicuddy and I have been married, I have never spoken one harsh word to her."

When Frank Demaree's baseball career ended, he and Nadine returned to California, where Frank worked his father's fruit farm and later became a technician at United Artists studios.

Cincinnati first baseman Les Scarsella's wife, Ann, did the play-by-play on radio station WCPO for one game in 1939. The next year, Les and Ann were driving with their two-year-old daughter, Elaine, down to spring training when their car collided with a coal truck. The child survived, as did Les, but Ann was killed.

Pitcher Milt Gaston's wife, Pearl, with her sister, Marie Harty, who also married a ballplayer, pitcher Danny MacFayden.

Mildred Dickey was the wife of White Sox catcher George "Skeets" Dickey and sister-in-law of Yankees catcher Bill Dickey. Mildred traveled from her hometown of Little Rock, Arkansas, to watch George play at Comiskey Park. "Every day was a holiday," she remembered.

Fathers and Sons

Cubs General Manager Bill Veeck Sr. taught the business to his son, Bill Jr. The younger Veeck, however, made up his own rules as owner of three American League clubs, sending a midget to the plate in St. Louis, hiring the league's first black player in Cleveland, and building the exploding scoreboard in Chicago. He once wrote: "Sometime, somewhere, there will be a club nobody really wants. And then Ol' Will will come wandering along to laugh some more. Look for me under the arc lights, boys. I'll be back."

Lon Warneke wore his 1933 National League All-Star uniform back home for a portrait with his father, Luke, a farmer in Mount Ida, Arkansas.

Cubs infielder Billy Herman with his son Billy Jr. in the team's dugout. Billy Jr. lived his whole life in his father's hometown, New Albany, Indiana, working for a railroad.

Hard-drinking slugger Hack Wilson, shown with son Bobby, was rejected by his wife in his later years. When he died in 1948, his body went unclaimed for two days until the National League paid $350 for his burial and a headstone. Bobby grew up to be a school principal in Martinsburg, West Virginia, and revered the memory of his father.

Thornton Lee was a White Sox pitcher when son Don came to visit in the early 1940s. A generation later, retired Thornton Lee visited his son Don, who was trying out for the Sox. The younger Lee pitched for six big league teams but not the White Sox.

Gabby Hartnett gives tips to his son Charles Jr. The boy later made it to the high minor leagues, playing for the Jersey City Giants. "My father told me I would never make it to the majors, so I said OK."

Sox outfielder Jocko Conlon puts son John on a pedestal at Comiskey Park. After two years in the majors, Jocko figured he might be a better umpire than player. He was right, and he was admitted to the Hall of Fame as an ump in 1974. John became a lawyer in Arizona.

Pitcher "Sad Sam" Jones with his sons George and Paul. Paul grew up to become an engineer. George, now retired from his job on Wall Street, remembers playing with toy cars on top of the White Sox dugout. He says he still has the uniform he wore in this picture.

Joey Kuhel, son of White Sox first baseman Joe Kuhel, chokes up on the bat. The younger Kuhel made it to the minor leagues as a pitcher and later became a Dallas businessman. "It was a great life for a kid," he recalls. "It was like being at a state fair every day."

Rip Radcliff's son, Raymond Jr., wears tough-guy intensity on his face and sissy shoes on his feet. Now a business consultant in Texas, he goes by his father's nickname, Rip.

Brothers

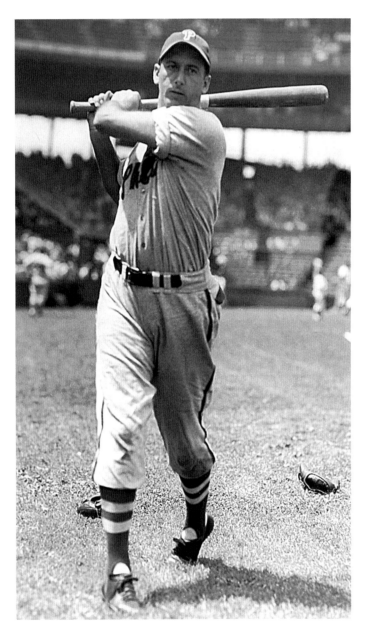 

Harry "the Hat" Walker and Fred "Dixie" Walker each won a batting title. Dixie's image slid, though, when he demanded a trade rather than play with Jackie Robinson.

Rick Ferrell (far left) was a catcher, brother Wes Ferrell was a pitcher, and in the 1930s they were teammates with the Boston Red Sox. Rick was older, but Wes made it to the majors first. Though Wes was a pitcher, he had more home runs than Rick. Wes was voted baseball's most handsome player; Rick wasn't. But Rick made the Hall of Fame; Wes didn't.

During a Dodgers intrasquad game, pitcher Larry Sherry (above) brushed back his brother Norm. "Do that again and I'll call Mom," said Norm.

There were three fine outfielders named DiMaggio, and all had their moments in All-Star Games. In the 1941 game, youngest brother Dom (above) singled in Joe (below). In 1943, oldest brother Vince (right) went three for three with a ninth-inning homer. In the 1949 All-Star Game, Joe returned an eight-year-old favor, knocking in Dom for a key run.

In 1934, Dizzy Dean made the outrageous prediction that "me 'n' Paul" would win 45 games as Cardinals pitchers. Instead, they won 49, plus four in the World Series.

The 1938 Yankees take aim. They are Lou Gehrig, Joe Gordon, Tommy Henrich, Joe DiMaggio, and Bill Dickey. The team won 99 games in the regular season to capture the American League pennant and went on to beat the Cubs in four straight World Series games.

"*Baseball is not precisely a team sport. It is more a series of concerts by the artists.*"

—SPORTSWRITER JIM MURRAY

LINEUPS

Burke and Brace loved group photos. They took team pictures at the first All-Star Game in 1933 and enjoyed pairing up players.

The National League wore a custom uniform for the first All-Star Game, held at Comiskey Park as part of festivities surrounding Chicago's 1933 Century of Progress Exposition. Not enough uniforms were ordered; batting-practice pitcher Bill Walker had to wear his Cardinals clothes. Pictured are (front row, from left) batboy Gil Hasbrook, Pepper Martin, Lon Warneke, Tony Cuccinello, (second row) Bill Hallahan, Dick Bartell, Bill Terry, coach Bill McKechnie, manager John McGraw, coach Max Carey, Chick Hafey, Chuck Klein, Lefty O'Doul, Wally Berger, (back row) Gabby Hartnett, Jimmy Wilson, Frankie Frisch, Carl Hubbell, Walker, Paul Waner, Woody English, Hal Schumacher, Pie Traynor, and trainer Andy Lotshaw.

The American League All-Stars, appearing in individual team uniforms, beat the Nationals 4–2. Babe Ruth hit the first home run in All-Star history, and starting pitcher Lefty Gomez was credited with the win. Pictured are (front row, from left) trainer Ad Schacht, coach Eddie Collins, Tony Lazzeri, General Crowder, Jimmie Foxx, Elbie Fletcher, Earl Averill, Eddie Rommel, Ben Chapman, Rick Ferrell, Sammy West, Charlie Gehringer, batting-practice pitcher Ken McBride, (back row) a clubhouse boy, a batboy, Lou Gehrig, Ruth, Oral Hildebrand, manager Connie Mack, Joe Cronin, Lefty Grove, a clubhouse boy, Bill Dickey, Al Simmons, Gomez, Wes Ferrell, Jimmy Dykes, and a clubhouse boy.

Rudy York and Hank Greenberg combined for more than 600 home runs in their careers. The Tigers had trouble finding a position for York, a lackluster fielder, so in 1940 they moved him to first base and paid first baseman Greenberg a $10,000 bonus to switch to left field.

Although they never played together, Pie Traynor was coach Honus Wagner's hitting pupil during the 1920s and his boss as the Pirates' manager during the 1930s.

The Boston Braves' motto "Spahn and Sain and pray for rain" worked in 1948 as Warren Spahn won

15 games and Johnny Sain won 24. The team won the pennant but lost the Series.

The great Cardinals outfield of Enos Slaughter, Terry Moore, and Joe Medwick. Each man batted over .300 in 1940. Slaughter and Medwick were later inducted into the Hall of Fame.

Men with Mitts

Four Cardinals catchers in 1939: Herman Franks, Mickey Owen, Don Padgett, and Sam Narron. Franks was a rookie, Owen was the team's regular catcher, Padgett also played the outfield, and Narron only caught a seat on the bench, appearing in no games for St. Louis that year.

Ernie Lombardi, "the Schnozz," was considered the slowest runner in baseball history. Opponents would play him so far back that he once said, "It took me four years to find out Pee Wee Reese was an infielder." Despite that, he was the only catcher to win two batting titles.

Clyde Sukeforth spent 10 years as a catcher with the Reds and Dodgers. Later, he was sent by Branch Rickey to scout Jackie Robinson and managed the Dodgers for one game, on April 15, 1947, when Robinson made his debut. The Dodgers won.

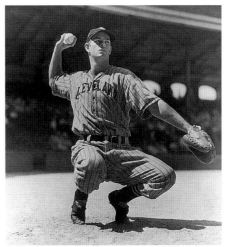

Indians catchers Henry Helf (above) and Frankie Pytlak each caught a baseball tossed from the 52nd story of Cleveland's Terminal Tower in 1938. The balls were dropped 708 feet by third baseman Ken Keltner. Said Pytlak, "It stung more than Bob Feller's fastball."

Gabby Street (above) caught a baseball dropped 555 feet from the top of the Washington Monument on a windy day in 1908 on his 15th try. Arrangements were made for him to catch a ball dropped from the 984-foot Eiffel Tower during World War I, but an injury canceled the stunt.

Future Managers

Cardinals manager Red Schoendienst began his 50 years in uniform as a second baseman in the National League. He started and finished his playing career with the Cardinals.

Los Angeles Dodgers manager Tommy Lasorda lost his only four decisions as a pitcher in a major league career lasting little more than three years with the Brooklyn Dodgers and Kansas City Athletics. He was dropped by the Dodgers to make way for a kid named Koufax.

Dodger manager Walter Alston came to bat once in the majors. He pinch hit for Johnny Mize after Mize was ejected from a game in 1936. Alston struck out.

Reds and Tigers manager Sparky Anderson played 152 games in his 1959 rookie season as a second baseman. He once held the record for the fewest total bases and lowest slugging percentage for any player who played in so many games. He never played in the majors again.

Don Zimmer's 12-year playing career was interrupted often by beanball injuries. Twice after beanings in the minor leagues, Zimmer was operated on to relieve pressure on the brain. He still has a steel plate in his head, a reminder of the lumps he took as a player.

Ralph Houk, who managed the Yankees, Tigers, and Red Sox, was a second-string catcher who hardly had use for batting practice. He appeared in only 91 games during his eight years as a Yankees player starting in 1947.

Sluggers

Graceful Johnny Mize hit home runs in bunches. Related to Babe Ruth through marriage—and power—"the Big Cat" was the only player to hit three homers in a game six times. In addition, he also smacked a pair of homers in 30 games.

"Cadillacs are down at the end of the bat," said Ralph Kiner in explaining why he didn't choke up. Kiner led the National League in homers in each of his first seven years. He finished with one of the highest home run percentages of all time.

The Phillies were so weak during the 1930s that it was rumored that a local newspaper had a standing headline that read "Klein Hits Two as Phils Lose." Chuck Klein, "the Hoosier Hammerer," was named the National League's most valuable player in 1932 and won the triple crown in 1933. The following year, he was traded to the Cubs and never again won a title.

Ted Kluszewski used to cut his shirt
sleeves to show off his muscles.
"Klu," who finished with a lifetime
average close to .300, was one of the
most controlled power swingers in
the history of the game. In 1954, he
hit 49 home runs and struck out only
35 times.

Ahead of the Game

Roger Craig invented the split-fingered fastball, a sinking forkball that shook up the game in the 1980s. Craig, who first taught it at a boys' camp in 1974 and then coached it to major leaguers, surely could have used it during his playing days. Breaking in with the Dodgers, he was cast off to the New York Mets. He lost 24 and 22 games during the team's first two seasons, becoming the first pitcher to lead the league in losses in consecutive years.

Rip Sewell's "eephus" pitch, a high, floating blooper, made him one of the game's biggest pitching stars during the war years. Sewell, who first shot-put the ball in 1942, used the pitch three straight times against Ted Williams in the 1946 All-Star Game. Williams took the first pitch, fouled off the second, and hit the third for a three-run homer.

George Blaeholder was the first pitcher to throw the slider. In 1928, he introduced the pitch, which starts as a fastball but curves just before it crosses the plate. It became a mainstay for pitchers during the 1950s. Blaeholder lost more games than he won in his 11-year career.

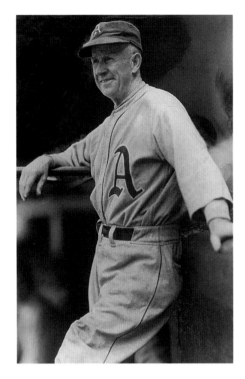

William "Kid" Gleason, manager of the 1919 Black Sox and later a coach for the Philadelphia Athletics, made his mark in 1896 by calling for baseball's first intentional walk. Gleason, captain of the New York Giants, told pitcher Jouett Meekin to walk Chicago Colts slugger Jimmy Ryan in order to get to weak hitter George Decker. Decker struck out to end the game.

Umpire Bill Klem popularized the ball-and-strike hand signals and the inside chest protector. Klem, considered the greatest umpire in baseball history, was so good he was cheered by fans.

Pitcher Phil "Flip" Paine became the
first major leaguer to play in Japan,
debuting there in 1953 while on leave
from the air force. He returned to the
majors and finished his stateside
career with 10 wins and only 1 loss.

Bruce Edwards was baseball's first
catcher to use a one-handed style,
protecting his bare hand behind his
back as he caught. The style has
lengthened the careers of many
catchers.

Money Players

Hack Wilson greets Chicago businessmen in 1930 after taking the major league home run lead from Babe Ruth. Wilson sold his bat that day to H. A. Sellen for $100.

Outfielder Edd Roush was one of the game's greatest holdouts. He sat out for much of the 1922 season with the Reds and the 1927 season with the Giants. In 1930, he boycotted the entire season. A .323 lifetime hitter who played much of his career in the dead-ball era, Roush was inducted into the Hall of Fame.

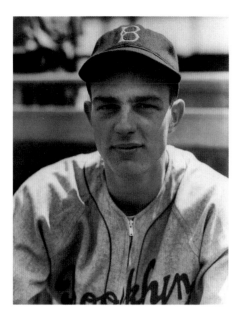

Outfielder Dick Wakefield was
baseball's first bonus baby. He was
given $52,000 to sign a contract with
the Tigers after graduating from the
University of Michigan in 1941. He
batted .316 during his first full season
but came back from military service
without his golden swing. Earlier,
Wakefield had been photographed by
Brace during a tryout with the
Brooklyn Dodgers, a team for which
he never played.

Danny Gardella filed the first lawsuit against baseball's reserve clause. The outfielder refused a $4,500 contract from the Giants and joined the Mexican League for $10,000. His defection earned him a five-year suspension from the majors, prompting Gardella to take legal action. Worried about the outcome, baseball officials agreed to pay Gardella $29,000 and lift his suspension. He returned for one at-bat with the Cardinals in 1950.

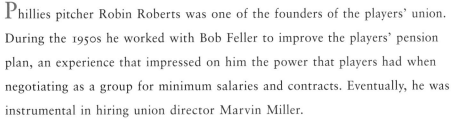

Phillies pitcher Robin Roberts was one of the founders of the players' union. During the 1950s he worked with Bob Feller to improve the players' pension plan, an experience that impressed on him the power that players had when negotiating as a group for minimum salaries and contracts. Eventually, he was instrumental in hiring union director Marvin Miller.

Tough Guys

Before he coached the Boston Braves, pitcher "Fat Freddie" Fitzsimmons was a mean mainstay of the Giants and Dodgers. Said Billy Herman: "He once hit me in the on-deck circle."

"Why is it there are so many nice guys interested in baseball?" asked Burleigh Grimes, the last man to throw a legal spitter. "Not me. I was a real bastard when I played."

Early Wynn, when asked if he would throw at his own mother: "It would depend on how well she was hitting."

"My own little rule was two for one," said Don Drysdale. "If one of my teammates got knocked down, then I knocked down two on the other team."

"I couldn't stop throwing the knockdown," said Sal "the Barber" Maglie. "That would be the same as if Marilyn Monroe stopped wearing sweaters."

Pitcher Johnny Allen reveled in his rotten reputation. He gave a cold stare to children who asked him for his autograph and was thoroughly disliked on the field. "He was just plain mean," said Lou Boudreau. "He wanted to hit the batter every time he had the ball in his hands."

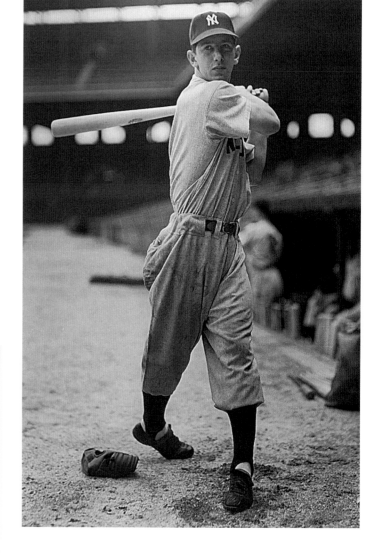

Billy Martin: "The day I become a good loser, I'm quitting baseball."

Lew Burdette intimidated batters with his wicked spitball. Red Smith of the *New York Times* once wrote that newspapers needed three columns for Burdette's statistics: wins, losses, and relative humidity.

Eddie "the Brat" Stanky was praised by Branch Rickey: "He can't hit, he can't run, he can't field, he can't throw. He can't do a goddamn thing . . . but beat you."

Underrated

Riggs Stephenson ended his 14-year career with the Cubs and Indians with a .336 lifetime average, the highest average of any non–Hall of Famer with more than 4,000 at-bats in the modern era except Shoeless Joe Jackson of the infamous Black Sox.

Babe Herman, the "Clown Prince"
of the Brooklyn Dodgers' Daffiness
Boys, stretched his major league
career from 1926 to 1945 on four
clubs. Although jokes were made of
his fielding and base running ability,
the outfielder finished with a .324
average.

Frank "Lefty" O'Doul came to the Giants at age 31 after being one of the top
hitters in the Pacific Coast League during the 1920s. In his 11-year major league
career, he led the National League in hitting twice and finished with a
remarkable .349 lifetime average.

Going Hollywood

Bob Uecker, shown on the minor league Indianapolis Indians in 1960, played six years in the majors. He became a sports commentator and the star of the TV show *Mr. Belvedere*. Another claim to fame: he hit two homers off Sandy Koufax.

Joe Garagiola likes to put down his baseball ability, but he was on his way to the 1950 All-Star Game when a shoulder separation slowed his career. Garagiola wrote a bestselling book about baseball and put together a long career as a sports commentator and TV host.

Johnny Berardino was known as a pretty boy during his playing years. As a publicity stunt, Browns owner Bill Veeck Jr. insured Berardino's face for $1 million. Transforming himself into John Beradino following his retirement, he played Dr. Steve Hardy in the soap opera *General Hospital* for more than 25 years.

"You can take the Hollywood fame, the house, everything," said Chuck Connors. "Just let me play baseball." Connors, a first baseman for the Dodgers and Cubs, went on to play the title role in TV's *The Rifleman* from 1957 to 1962 and appear on other TV shows and in movies.

Spectacles

George "Specs" Toporcer, shown during his minor league days, was one of the first players to come up to the majors wearing glasses. He played for eight years as a utility infielder for the Cardinals. Many years after his playing career was over, Toporcer went blind.

Ryne Duren's bad eyesight, wild fastball, and drinking habits made batters and fans take notice. Said Casey Stengel of "Blind Ryne": "Whenever he came into a game, people would stop eating their popcorn."

Reliever Jim Konstanty left the Braves for the Phillies, where in 1950 he led the Whiz Kids to the pennant. He became the first player with glasses to win the Most Valuable Player Award. He was also the first relief pitcher to be named MVP.

Outfielder Chick Hafey was the first batting champion to wear glasses, hitting .349 for the St. Louis Cardinals in 1931. He is shown in his 1933 National League All-Star uniform.

Crossing the Color Line

The first African Americans to play on each of the major league teams were usually not stars. After Jackie Robinson broke into the National League and Larry Doby entered the American League in 1947, it took 12 more years for the last team, the Red Sox, to integrate.

Monte Irvin,
New York Giants.

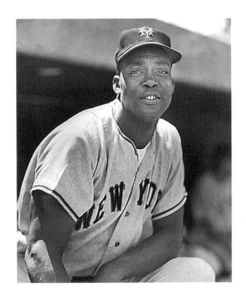

Elston Howard,
New York Yankees.

Larry Doby, Cleveland Indians.

The Dodgers' Dan Bankhead, baseball's first black pitcher and the first black player to hit a home run in the majors.

Jackie Robinson, Brooklyn Dodgers.

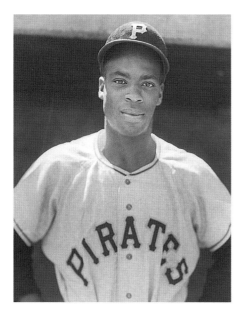

Curt Roberts, Pittsburgh Pirates.

Henry Thompson, St. Louis Browns.

Tom Alston, St. Louis Cardinals.

John Kennedy, Philadelphia Phillies, shown late in his career when he was in the minor leagues.

Minnie Minoso, Chicago White Sox.

Carlos Paula, Washington Senators.

Nino Escalera, Cincinnati Reds.

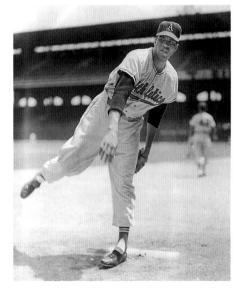

Bob Trice, Kansas City Athletics.

Sam Jethroe, Boston Braves.

Ossie Virgil Sr., Detroit Tigers.

Ernie Banks, Chicago Cubs.

Pumpsie Green, Boston Red Sox.

The Name Game

Ernest "Blimp" Phelps.

"Fat Pat" Seerey.

Joe "Muscles" Gallagher.

Robert "Fatty" Fothergill.

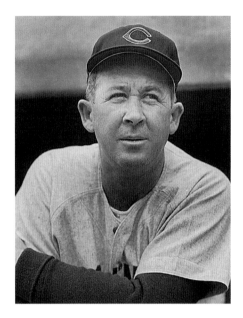

George "Birdie" Tebbets.

George "Mule" Haas.

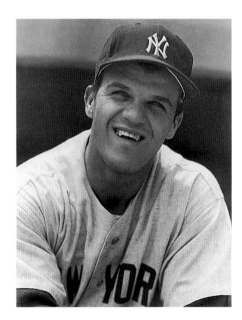

Bill "Moose" Skowron.

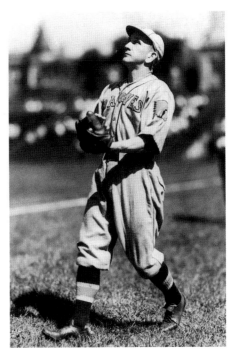

Walter "Rabbit" Maranville.

Leon "Goose" Goslin.

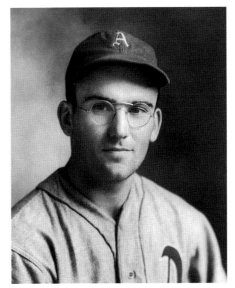

William "Bullfrog" Dietrich.

Nicholas "Dim Dom" Dallessandro.

Charles "King Kong" Keller.

Sheldon "Available" Jones.

Art "What-a-Man" Shires.

Anatomy of a Ballplayer

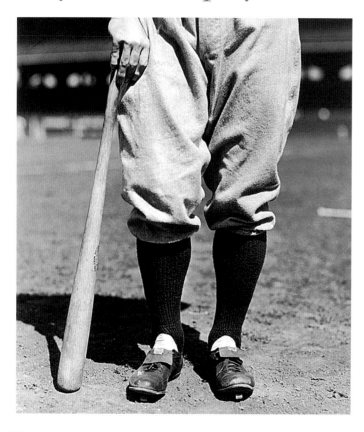

"Lou Gehrig had the most powerful legs in baseball," says George Brace. That is why this picture, among the dozens he took of Gehrig, is his favorite.

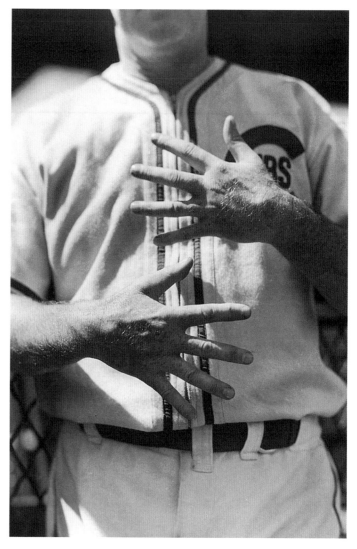

Gabby Hartnett was proud to show his unbroken fingers, which were unusual for a catcher of his era.

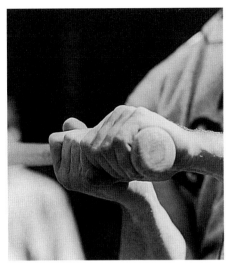

The powerful batting grip of "Double X," Jimmie Foxx.

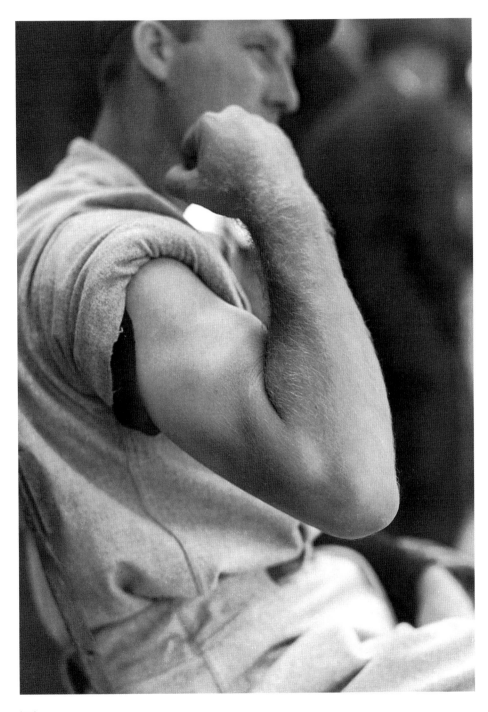

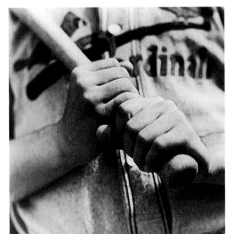

"Ducky" Medwick was a hit when he met the pope during World War II: "Your Holiness, I'm Joseph Medwick. I, too, used to be a Cardinal."

The rugged right arm of Yankees Hall of Fame pitcher Red Ruffing.

There really was a Van Lingle Mungo. The Dodgers
pitcher went by the name of Van Mungo during his
playing career, but singer Dave Frishberg added
Mungo's middle name when he wrote "Van Lingle
Mungo," his 1970 bossa nova classic, which recalled
the great player names of the '30s and '40s. The real
Mungo was an unlikely subject for warm nostalgia.
He had a drinking problem and a ferocious temper.
Said his manager, Casey Stengel, "Mungo and I get
along fine. I just tell him I won't stand for no
nonsense—and then I duck."

"Don't anybody ever

get into trouble but me?"

—Van Lingle Mungo,
AFTER A HOTEL-ROOM BRAWL

MORTALS

*They're seldom in the record books—some belong in
the funny papers, while others belong in the rap
sheets. Their stories are sad, strange, and surprising,
just like the game itself.*

Bad Bounces

Russell "Buzz" Arlett was one of the greatest minor leaguers of all time: a 20-game winner as a pitcher who switched to the outfield and hit .341 lifetime. He finally reached the majors in 1931 with the Phillies, batting .313 and finishing fourth in the league in home runs. But his fielding was atrocious, and when the season ended, he was back to the minors for good.

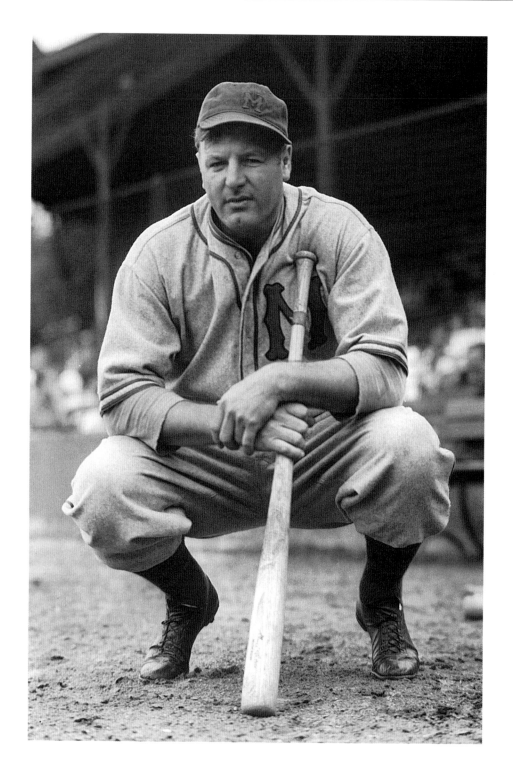

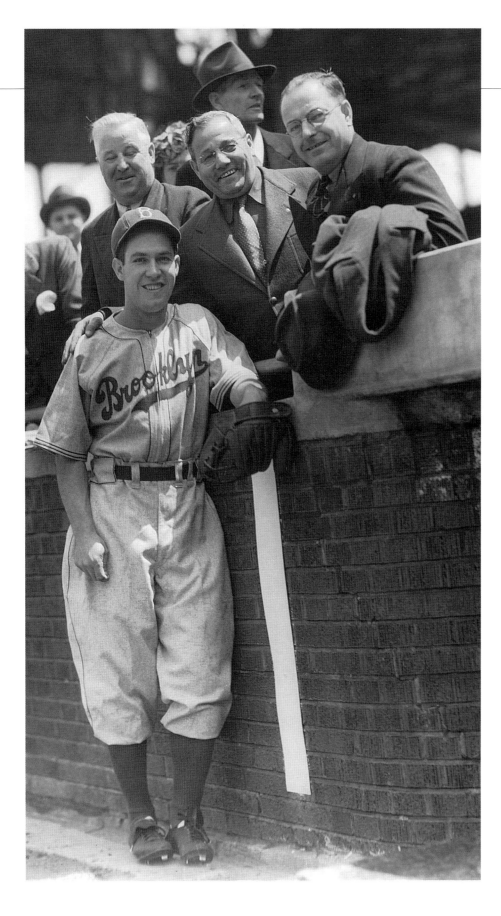

Dodger center fielder Pete Reiser won the batting title in his first full season, 1941, but also led the league in broken collarbones, dislocated shoulders, and fractured skulls. He was carried off the field 11 times in his career. His scariest injury came in 1947, when he forgot that the Ebbets Field center-field fence had been moved in 40 feet. He hit the fence at a full sprint, collapsed, and was carried into the clubhouse, where a priest administered the last rites. Reiser was paralyzed for 10 days, but he recovered to play five more seasons. "Reiser had great potential," says Brace. "But he just kept running into fences."

Alva "Bobo" Holloman's first start in the majors was spectacular: he pitched a no-hitter for the Browns, had two hits of his own, and drove in three runs. But he finished the 1953 season with a 3–7 record, never got another hit, and was out of the majors by the next year.

Gene "Half-Pint" Rye once had three home runs and seven RBI in one inning. But that was in the minors, for Waco in the Texas League in 1930. Rye's stint in the majors was far less impressive: a .179 batting average in 17 games for the Red Sox. Brace photographed Rye when he played for the semipro Chicago Mills.

Joe Nuxhall, called up to the majors at age 15, pitched two-thirds of an inning for the 1944 wartime Reds, giving up two hits, five walks, and five runs. He was sent back to the minors and didn't return until 1952. As he later told reporters, it took him eight years to get that third out.

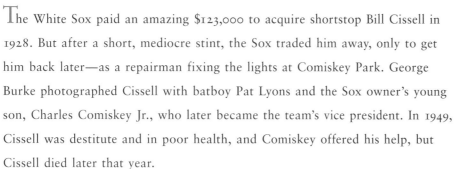

The White Sox paid an amazing $123,000 to acquire shortstop Bill Cissell in 1928. But after a short, mediocre stint, the Sox traded him away, only to get him back later—as a repairman fixing the lights at Comiskey Park. George Burke photographed Cissell with batboy Pat Lyons and the Sox owner's young son, Charles Comiskey Jr., who later became the team's vice president. In 1949, Cissell was destitute and in poor health, and Comiskey offered his help, but Cissell died later that year.

You Could Look It Up

Virgil "Fire" Trucks pitched five shutouts, including two no-hitters, for the Tigers in 1952 but still had a lousy year: he lost his other 19 decisions.

Pitcher George "Hard Head" Uhle got his nickname in the late 1920s when he started a double play with his head. A line drive hit him on the skull and bounced in the air to the catcher, who threw for the second out. Brace later got a photo of Uhle with announcer Jim Dudley.

As a pitcher for the Athletics in 1934, Al Benton faced Babe Ruth. As a Red Sox pitcher in 1952, he faced Mickey Mantle. Both homered off him.

Carroll Hardy, a lifetime .225 hitter, pinch hit for Ted Williams, Roger Maris, and Carl Yastrzemski. Hardy was the only man ever to replace Williams at bat. He came in after Williams was injured fouling a ball off his foot.

Hall of Fame knuckleballer Hoyt Wilhelm hit a home run in his first major league at-bat. In 21 years in the majors, he never hit another one.

Because Brace took photographs of players every time they changed teams, his files are bulging with pictures of pitcher Bobo Newsom, who switched major league uniforms 15 times. The Washington Senators traded for Newsom five times, purportedly because owner Clark Griffith needed a fourth for bridge.

Knuckleball pitchers are rare now, but in 1945 the Senators had four in their starting rotation and finished one game out of first place. Not surprisingly, Senators catcher Rick Ferrell led the league in passed balls.

Roger Wolff: 20 wins, 10 losses.

Mickey Haefner: 16 wins, 14 losses.

Johnny Niggeling: 7 wins, 12 losses.

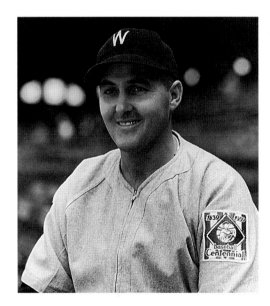

Dutch Leonard: 17 wins, 7 losses.

Tough Losses

Cincinnati backup catcher Willard Hershberger was especially moody after he went 0 for 5 on August 2, 1940. He called in sick the next day and was found dead in his hotel room, having killed himself by slashing his throat with a razor blade. The reason was never established. Manager Bill McKechnie, who had counseled Hershberger, said, "I know what happened, but I'm going to my grave with it." And he did.

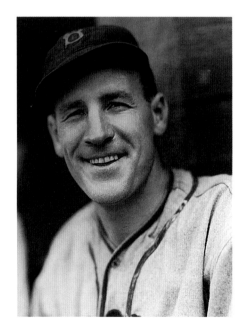

Dodgers outfielder Len Koenecke was drunk when he boarded a small plane from Detroit to New York near the end of the 1935 season. Somewhere over Toronto, Koenecke started nudging the pilot and rocking the plane. The pilot and copilot fought with him, finally clobbering him with a fire extinguisher to subdue him. After the plane made an emergency landing in Toronto, Koenecke was declared dead.

Former Red Sox pitcher Gordon McNaughton, 10 years out of baseball, was in a Chicago hotel room with a woman in 1942 when he was confronted by another woman, Eleanor Williams. She shot him to death. As police led Williams away, she said, "I'm glad I shot him."

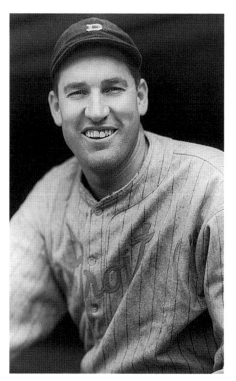

Dale "Moose" Alexander of the Red Sox won the American League batting title in 1932. The next year, he hurt his knee sliding home. The trainer used an electric current to heat the knee but forgot to check the machine and burned Alexander. "I ended up with third-degree burns and a gangrene infection and almost lost my leg," he said. "I was finished in the majors."

Eddie Waitkus was on the Phillies when he was shot at Chicago's Edgewater Beach Hotel in 1949. Waitkus, a bachelor, was stalked and wounded by 19-year-old Ruth Ann Steinhagen, who'd had a crush on him since his days with the Cubs. Though she shot him, Steinhagen remained an admirer, saying, "He showed so much courage as he lay there on the floor. The way he looked up at me and kept smiling." Waitkus returned to the majors the next season, winning the Comeback of the Year Award. The shooting scene in *The Natural* was inspired by this event.

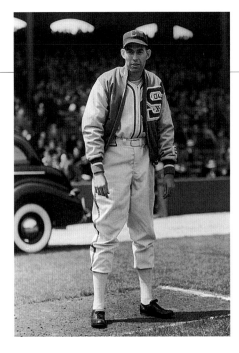

Monty Stratton was a promising White Sox starter who posted a 30–14 record over the 1937 and 1938 seasons. Then he went rabbit hunting and his pistol accidentally discharged and he lost a leg. Fitted with an artificial limb, Stratton attempted a comeback, pitching an exhibition game against the Cubs in Comiskey Park. Stratton threw hard and the crowd cheered harder, but it was clear his major league career was over. "It was the saddest day I ever remember in baseball," says Brace.

Herb Score led the American League in strikeouts in his first two seasons with the Indians. Then, in 1957, he was struck in the eye by a line drive hit by the Yankees' Gil McDougald. He tried a comeback over the next five years but never again posted a winning record. He has remained with the Indians, announcing their games, ever since.

Julius "Moose" Solters, a veteran American League outfielder, was waving to a relative during warm-ups at Griffith Stadium in Washington, D.C., when he was hit in the face by a thrown ball. Solters battled back from the injury, but it eventually caused him to go blind.

Major league prospect Bert Shepard went off to fight in World War II, suffered a leg wound, and was taken prisoner by the Germans. After his right leg was amputated, he was fitted with an artificial leg. Shepard returned from the war and pitched five and one-third innings for the Senators against the Red Sox. He gave up only three hits and threw out two hitters on grounders, but he knew his career was over.

Notorious

Yankees outfielder Jake Powell, in a 1938 radio interview, made a racially offensive remark, which caused an uproar. As part of his penance, Powell went to Harlem by himself after dark, walked into bar after bar, announced who he was, and bought everyone a drink. Ten years later, he was arrested in Washington, D.C., for passing bad checks. As officers watched in shock, Powell pulled out a gun in the middle of the police station and shot himself to death.

Ben Chapman was a first-string bigot. As a player, he slid into and tried to injure Jewish infielder Buddy Myer and was forced to leave the Yankees because of anti-Semitic remarks. As manager of the Phillies, Chapman encouraged his players to harass Jackie Robinson. In one game, Chapman threw a black cat onto the field to try to unnerve baseball's black pioneer. Chapman was made to apologize and was fired the next year.

One day in 1945, St. Louis Browns pitcher Sig Jakucki was asked by one-armed player Pete Gray to help him tie his shoes. Jakucki's answer: "Tie your own goddamned shoes, you one-armed son of a bitch."

Strange but True

Wrigley Field wasn't exactly the "Friendly Confines" to Lou Novikoff (right). A star minor leaguer, Novikoff got spooked by the major league park, declaring that the left-field foul line was crooked and the outfield wall had poison ivy. Once, he stole third base with the bases loaded, later explaining that he had done so because "I got such a good jump on the pitcher."

Richie Ashburn (left) used to sleep with his Louisville Slugger during a slump. "I wanted to know my bat a little better," said the star of the Phillies' Whiz Kids.

The saying at the time was "Moe Berg can speak 12 languages, but he can't hit in any of them." Casey Stengel called the third-string catcher "the strangest fella who ever put on a uniform." When Babe Ruth and Lou Gehrig went on a players' tour of Japan in 1934, Berg went along, but he had a secret mission: to take reconnaissance photos of Tokyo. The photos later were used in World War II bombing missions. Berg retired in 1939 to join the Office of Strategic Services, precursor of the CIA.

Henry Grampp (left) appeared in only three games during the 1920s, but as a batting-practice pitcher in the '30s he was the Cubs' secret weapon. Brace says Grampp could imitate the style of any opposing pitcher, both righty and lefty, and he went so far as to use putty and paint his face so he looked *and* pitched like the upcoming opponent.

Pitcher Flint Rhem (right) was an all-star drunk. Caught boozing with Grover Cleveland Alexander, Rhem told his coach: "I was only trying to drink his share to keep him sober." After missing an important game during the Cardinals' 1930 pennant drive, Rhem had a ready alibi: he had been kidnapped and forced to drink whiskey at gunpoint.

Pitcher Moe Drabowsky was the king of prank phone calls. He once called Brooks Robinson during a Baltimore radio broadcast and imitated Kansas City owner Charles Finley, telling Robinson he had been traded. Impersonating Kansas City manager Alvin Dark, he once called the bullpen during a game and got a reliever to start warming up.

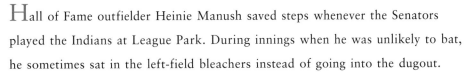

Hall of Fame outfielder Heinie Manush saved steps whenever the Senators played the Indians at League Park. During innings when he was unlikely to bat, he sometimes sat in the left-field bleachers instead of going into the dugout.

Jimmy Piersall's mental health seemed to flutter in the outfield wind. His nervous breakdown in 1952 was a prelude to a career of antics that spanned 15 years. "He was a pleasure to be with most of the time, telling great stories about baseball and about his kids," Brace says, "but then he would turn around and get mad for no reason at all." Piersall would bring a can of bug spray with him to the outfield, and he ran around the bases backward after his 100th career home run. Casey Stengel couldn't tolerate him on the Mets, declaring, "There's room for only one clown on this team."

Frenchy Bordagaray was fined $500 and suspended 60 days for spitting at an ump. Said he: "The penalty is a bit more than I expectorated."

_S_econds after the final out as the Cubs beat the Reds 11–5 during the 1930s. As the players walk off, a few kids hop out of the bleachers for a run in the outfield sun.

"In each fan's heart lurks the hope that a home run with the bases loaded will climax the game in victory for the home team. How rarely that happens, you know. Yet we are incurably romantic, ever chasing rainbows, and in baseball we find our pot of gold at the end of a home run."

—George Brace

SOURCES

This book's primary source, of course, has been George Brace and his amazing photo collection. Brace is an unassuming man who has not boasted about or promoted his work. He does not advertise or demand recognition even with a photo credit line. People who have come across the collection over the years have generally kept their find to themselves.

Brace is one of the last great links to the Babe Ruth era. He remembers the names of almost all of his 10,000 subjects and recognizes most of their faces. He also remembers personalities and describes the old players in words as well as pictures.

Richard Cahan, picture editor at the *Chicago Sun-Times*, jotted down Brace's name several years ago when he kept coming across the name stamped on the back of old baseball photographs. Finally, Cahan called Brace out of curiosity. Brace invited Cahan to see the pictures during the first week of the 1994 baseball season. That first day, Brace showed him negatives of Lou Gehrig and Willie Mays and gave him a small stack of prints to take home and study. Cahan soon invited his friend, Mark Jacob, the *Sun-Times*' Sunday editor, to see for himself.

The 1994 baseball season, derailed by the players strike, was the worst for most baseball fans. For Cahan and Jacob, however, it was the best season ever. They were transported back to an age when ballplayers could legally load up a spitball, a time when fans could stand on the outfield grass. Soon, the two were visiting Brace's collection often to go through the archive negative by negative. They didn't stop until they had seen it all. Suddenly, the statistics in the baseball abstracts and baseball encyclopedias came to life. And they were holding memories in their hands.

Brace's work, while little known in art and photography circles, has long been a valuable resource for baseball collectors—they order simple prints at bargain-basement prices. The negatives are meticulously organized by player and then by each of the player's teams. For example, Monte Irvin, who goes by Monford Merrill Irvin in Brace's system, has files for his minor league playing days, his New York Giants years, and his last year, which was with the Cubs. Brace keeps few prints. Negatives are viewed the old-fashioned way: they are held up to the nearest light because he has no light table and no magnifying glass. But the negatives are so large and lush that choices are easy to make.

Brace has also collected other people's photos of every ballplayer back to the turn of the century.

In addition, he has a fine baseball library, which includes copies or originals of almost every yearly major baseball guide in existence.

Quite a few of the envelopes that contain Brace's ballpark negatives have inadequate information on the people in the pictures. To identify those photographed, the authors have frequently relied on the *Chicago Sun-Times* library, which contains an extensive clipping file from that paper and from the defunct *Chicago Daily News*. Researchers at the National Baseball Library in Cooperstown, New York, were very helpful. Many other photographs were shown to ballplayers, team officials, sportswriters, and baseball fans.

Some captions required intensive detective work. Burke took a photo of a trainer working on a Pirates player, which appears on page 107. The photo was marked "Chas. A. Jorgenson," with no other identification. Brace remembered that Jorgenson was a trainer for several decades, but he could not identify the player in the photo. A look at the print through a magnifying glass showed that the three players behind the training table were sitting at lockers marked with the names of shortstop Arky Vaughan, pitcher Bill Swift, and coach Johnny Gooch. These men were on the Pirates together only one year, 1938. With this information, Brace perused the team roster and determined the player on the table was leftfielder Johnny Rizzo. A quick print of a negative in the player file confirmed it.

Another mystery was the photo of Glen Gorbous and Ron Negray on page 86. The only marking on the envelope read: "Beauty Queens." The players were obscure, even to Brace. Another

negative in the same folder showed the Wrigley Field scoreboard with all the teams. Two of the teams on the scoreboard were Kansas City and Brooklyn, so it was determined that the photo must have been taken sometime from 1955, Kansas City's first year, to 1957, Brooklyn's last year. Brace produced his schedules from the 1950s and found the date when all of the games on the scoreboard were going on. Again, the team roster was checked and Brace determined the players.

All of this work could not have been accomplished without the tremendous wealth of baseball literature. The authors consulted dozens of books, consistently stripping the 796 section of the Skokie, Illinois, Public Library. Favorites include the following:

The Baseball Encyclopedia: The Complete and Official Record of Major League Baseball (Macmillan, 1990) is considered by many baseball's essential stat manual.

Total Baseball: The Official Encyclopedia of Major League Baseball, edited by John Thorn and Pete Palmer (Viking Penguin, 1995), was a constant desk reference, full of stats as well as insightful articles on many aspects of the game. This is one of the few sources that includes a list of major league coaches. If you could own only one book on baseball history, this would be the one to choose.

The Ballplayers: Baseball's Ultimate Biographical Reference, edited by Mike Shatzkin (William Morrow, 1990), is the best biographical reference on the market. It profiles more than 5,000 players, providing details where stat books leave off. Where else can you find the cause of Jimmie Foxx's death (he choked on a piece of meat) or the amount of money Bill Veeck paid midget Eddie Gaedel ($100)?

Baseball When the Grass Was Real: Baseball from the Twenties to the Forties, Told by the Men Who Played It, by Donald Honig (University of Nebraska Press, 1993), gives the players' stories in their own words. It must have been difficult to write because it seems so easy to read. The book contains several Burke and Brace photos.

The Glory of Their Times: The Story of the Early Days of Baseball Told by the Men Who Played It, by Lawrence S. Ritter (Morrow, 1992), reminds us a great deal of Brace's work. Ritter saved the words of baseball's first great stars. Brace saved the images.

Baseball's Greatest Quotations: From Walt Whitman to Dizzy Dean, Garrison Keillor to Woody Allen, a Treasury of over 5000 Quotations Plus Historical Lore, Notes & Illustrations, by Paul Dickson (HarperCollins, 1992), is the most complete and accurate volume of baseball sayings, perfectly organized both for armchair reading and for research. Fans should check out the 18 pages of Stengelese.

Baseball Uniforms of the Twentieth Century: The Official Major League Baseball Guide, by Marc Okkonen (Sterling, 1993), is the secret weapon of the photo researcher. Baseball uniforms give many clues to the year and location a photo is taken. It is only fair that we used this book, because Brace's photos provided Okkonen with a great deal of help in his research.

The Bill James Historical Baseball Abstract, by Bill James and Mary A. Wirth (Villard Books, 1985), is as fun as it is comprehensive. This book separates baseball's decades better than any we have found and gives the reader a firm understanding of the changing game.

Baseball's Golden Age: The Photographs of Charles M. Conlon, by Neal McCabe and Constance McCabe (Harry N. Abrams, 1993), proves the idea that baseball photographs are fine art if printed with care. Don't ignore the captions; they are as poetic as the photographs.

Baseball Address List No. 8, by R. J. "Jack" Smalling (Edgewater Books, 1994), saves a serious baseball fan about 20 years of research. It contains the addresses of just about every living ballplayer.

The Membership Directory of the Society of American Baseball Research offers quick access to thousands of baseball experts around the world. The SABR members we called were very helpful in tracking down obscure information and photo IDs. One SABR member, a retiree from St. Louis by the name of Stan Musial, lists his expertise as "hitting a baseball."

INDEX